Contents

The Revd Samuel Frederick Leighton Green MC (1882–1929)

Introduction

On Saturday 1 June 1929, hundreds of people filed into All Saints, Mundesley, a small country church on the north-east coast of Norfolk, to pay their last respects to the late rector. When the church was full, those who couldn't gain admittance stood solemnly outside. The number of mourners alone would have been unusual for the funeral of a humble priest of an obscure rural parish. Even more extraordinary were the full military honours that were observed. His coffin, surrounded by candles and draped in a Union Jack, had lain in the chancel since Thursday evening, watched over by relays of veterans from the local branch of the British Legion. After the service, a party of soldiers bore his coffin to the grave where three volleys were fired and the Last Post and Reveille sounded. A few days later one of his former comrades wrote in the local paper that 'there would be many a London soldier who will grieve when they know that his Padre has "gone West"'.[1] Who then was this soldier priest, so beloved and admired?

Samuel Frederick Leighton Green was born at his parents' home, 71 Ashburnham Grove, Greenwich, on 6 April 1882. The world in which he grew up was probably not so very different from that depicted in the classic comic novel of lower middle-class, Victorian suburbia, *The Diary of a Nobody*, with its leafy avenues of terraced houses and modest villas rented by clerks and shopkeepers with incomes just sufficient, in a good year, to employ a sole female domestic to fetch and carry for the lady of the house. It was respectable but not quite the thing, and the young Sam Green, who was to call himself the Revd S. F. Leighton Green after ordination, was clearly keen to add some polish in a society where the clergy were still looked upon as minor gentry. His mother, born Catherine Robson in Bishop Auckland, County Durham, in 1843, was, unusually, thirteen years older than her husband and, at the age of 39, rather old by the standards of that era to be having her first child. His father, Frederick Charles Green, born in Hackney in 1856, was the younger son of William Green, a municipal official for the City of London Corporation, who held at one time the grandly titled post of High Constable and Inspector of Weights and Measures, Nuisances and Lamps, though his duties were essentially clerical. At the time of his birth his father was working as a civil service clerk in the Accountant General's department at the War Office, eventually rising to the rank of staff officer at the Royal Ordnance Factories in nearby Woolwich. He had one brother, Arthur John Bradford Green, a year his junior, who went up to Cambridge and became a schoolmaster at Guildford Royal Grammar School.

Green was educated at King's College School, which had been established in a basement in the Strand in 1831 as the junior department of King's College London. A fee-paying private school, it had a strong Anglican bias and religious education was given prominence. In 1897, during Green's final year, the school moved to more spacious premises in Wimbledon, which could not but have disrupted his education. Its abler pupils were expected to go on to King's College London; Green, however, left at 16 to begin work as a commercial clerk in a firm of ships' brokers in the City, following in the same clerical footsteps as his father, grandfather and uncle, William A. Green, who also worked as a commercial clerk, in London's docks. The commercial world clearly did not agree with him, however, for after a very few years he began to study for another type of clerical work, as a clerk in Holy Orders, at St Paul's Theological College in the University of London, passing his preliminary examinations first class in 1904.

Heigham clergy, *c.* 1905: Green (right), Revd C. C. Lanchester (second left), Revd D. W. Mountfield (seated)

His first appointment was in Norfolk, at St Bartholomew's, Heigham, a fifteenth-century parish church that found itself at the beginning of the twentieth century in the midst of a sprawling, working-class suburb of Norwich. He was licensed as an assistant curate here in June 1905 under the instruction of the rector, the Revd David Witts Mountfield, and was

6

ordained a deacon of the Church of England later that year. The following year, having successfully passed his probationary period, he was ordained a priest by the Bishop of Norwich, the Right Revd John Sheepshanks. He remained at St Bartholomew's until Easter 1912, when he was appointed assistant priest at St Bartholomew's daughter church, St Barnabas'. Here he came under the tutelage of its youthful and energetic vicar, the Revd Charles Compton Lanchester, a pioneer motorist who, remarkably, was to serve as priest here for sixty-four years. St Barnabas' was a young church; it had only been consecrated in 1906, built to help spread the load of the Anglican

St Barnabas', Heigham, not long after consecration in 1906

mission placed on St Bartholomew's in an area of Norwich with a rapidly growing population. Before it was built Bishop Sheepshanks had commented: 'The work of the Church must be inadequately carried out in a parish where the incumbent has a population of 12,000 souls, almost wholly poor, one very small church ... and one mission chapel'.[2] Within months of

7

Derby Street, Heigham, during the 1912 floods

his appointment Green faced perhaps the sternest task of his curacy so far with the devastating Norwich floods of August 1912. Virtually every house in the parish was inundated and St Barnabas' itself was under three and a half feet of water at the flood's height. Green and the vicar went around the parish in a rowing boat, true fishers of men, delivering food and fresh water to families marooned in their upstairs rooms. Thousands of poor families with few resources were left destitute, requiring a great deal of pastoral work in the community, as well as much fund-raising to help pay for essential repair work on the church. The vicar, no sentimentalist, commented that several of the homes in the parish, recipients of charitable donations of furniture, were better furnished after the flood than before it.[3]

Local calamities notwithstanding, many in the years to come would look back on these pre-war years as a golden age. Despite widespread poverty, the vicar always thought of it as a happy parish, with a community spirit more like a village than an industrial suburb. St Barnabas' parish magazine tells of Sunday School picnics, Church Lads' Brigade band concerts and summer outings for the local children and their parents, down the river by paddle steamer. War, when it came, brought with it a sense of fear and excitement. In the parish magazine, the Revd Lanchester wrote:

We are none of us likely to forget the solemn suspense that seemed to hang over us on the Bank Holiday Sunday and Monday, nor the thrill with which we heard on Tuesday morning [4 August] that the die was cast, and that we had begun to take part in what is probably the greatest war in the history of the world.[4]

Church bells were silenced. By night a blackout was ordered because of the threat of Zeppelin raids. Army and navy reservists and men who had already joined the Territorials were called up for duty immediately, while thousands of others rushed to volunteer, eager to take part in a war that many believed would be over by Christmas. By the end of the war, four weary years later, St Barnabas' and St Bartholomew's combined rolls of honour, with nearly 300 names, would top the list of Norwich parishes, accounting for over a tenth of all of the casualties suffered by the City. In the early months of the war, however, there was still a sense of optimism, of glorious deeds and noble

Norwich recruits marching down Unthank Road, 1914
[photo: Mildred Mary Swain]

enterprise against an ungodly and despicable foe. The majority of the clergy had no doubt that this was a just and righteous war, and many encouraged their former choir boys, communicants and Church Lads' Brigaders to volunteer, convinced that it was their Christian duty to defend the mother-

9

**Officers and NCOs of the 1st Battalion, Norwich Regiment, Church Lads'
Brigade, 1917: Revd Lanchester, assistant chaplain to the battalion,
standing fourth left; Revd G. N. Herbert, senior chaplain, seated first left**

land. The very structure of some of the Church's youth groups was based on
the ideals of military discipline and the chivalrous Christian warrior. St
Barnabas', for example, had a Ward of St George (a boys' confirmation club,
run by Green), while many Church Lads' Brigaders, because of their rifle
training, were recruited, sometimes under-age, straight into elite light
infantry regiments such as the King's Royal Rifle Corps.[5] In September
1914, the Dean of Norwich, the Very Revd H. C. Beeching, gave a sermon,
later published under the title *Armageddon,* in which he characterised the war
as a holy war 'of Christ against anti-Christ'.[6] About the same time he wrote
in the introduction to a collection of 'Patriotic Verse for Boys and Girls', *Our
Glorious Heritage,* that 'no Englishman who is true to his national history will
refuse to make the sacrifice of war'.[7] The Revd Lanchester echoed such
views, writing in the parish magazine: 'We face [the war] with confidence,
because we believe sincerely that our country's cause is a just and righteous
one'.[8]

Able-bodied clergy of military age who supported the war from the pulpit
were faced with the dilemma of whether or not to volunteer for active service
themselves. Some did, while others felt that even though the war was just, as
priests they could not contemplate the taking of human life themselves, a

10

The Very Revd H. C. Beeching, Dean of Norwich
[photo: G. M. Mason]
Britannia defending the motherland, front cover of *Our Glorious Heritage*

stance that laid them open to charges of cowardice and hypocrisy. Some decided to volunteer for the auxiliary medical services as an honourable and humane compromise. A year after the outbreak of war, the Revd Lanchester, then in his mid-forties, crossed to Boulogne to place his skills as a motorist at the disposal of a Red Cross ambulance brigade, writing a series of letters detailing his experiences. These were published monthly in the parish magazine, a tradition Green would carry on in his turn. Another option was to apply to become an army chaplain, though there were always many more candidates than places. In September 1915 Lanchester noted: 'There is no lack of chaplains out here, and very good men they are'. When the vicar returned to St Barnabas' at the end of the year, Green, who had taken on all of his duties during his absence, was finally free to volunteer for service as a chaplain; candidates had to have their bishop's permission to go and could not leave their parish unless there was another priest to carry on their duties.

The Army Chaplains' Department was established in 1796 as an integral part of the British Army. The Department had its own staff and headquarters, like any regular corps. Chaplains held the King's Commission and, with a few exceptions, were subject to the same rules and regulations as any officer. Chaplain to the Forces (CF) and Temporary Chaplain to the Forces (TCF) were regarded as roughly equivalent to an army captain, and those appointed wore the standard British officer's uniform, the main distinguishing features of which were the traditional clerical collar and stock, the Department's silver and black Maltese Cross lapel and cap badges and the fact that they carried no weapons. At the beginning of the war the Department had just over 100 full-time chaplains, of whom sixty-five went with the British Expeditionary Force (BEF) to France immediately. By the end of the war it had recruited over 4,400 chaplains, mostly TCFs, of whom 179 died on active service. Three were awarded the Victoria Cross. Their number was drawn from all the major Christian denominations, Anglican, Nonconformist and Roman Catholic, as well as from the Jewish faith, although the Church of England predominated, particularly in the higher ranks.

The imposing Chaplain-General, Bishop Taylor Smith

Having been passed medically fit, Green was interviewed on 18 January 1916 by the head of the Department, the Chaplain-General, Bishop John Taylor Smith.[9] Interviews with the Bishop were disconcerting affairs. Taylor Smith, a former missionary in Africa who, it was said, had only attained his exalted position because he had been one of Queen Victoria's favourite preachers, was possessed of an evangelical zeal, which he expected his subordinates to share wholeheartedly. Applicants would invariably be questioned closely on their understanding of the correct spiritual preparation of the dying, being asked, for example, what they would say or do to save the soul of a man who had three minutes to live. It was a situation that successful candidates would soon be experiencing under conditions very far from anything he could ever have imagined, including the appalling duty of accompanying soldiers convicted of cowardice or desertion to the execution post. Early in the war Taylor Smith had been accused by Lord Halifax, President of the English Church Union, of having an anti-High Church bias when it came to appointing chaplains. Taylor Smith responded by saying there was no room for extremists in the Army, which showed what he thought of the sacramentalists. As Green was decidedly on the Anglo-Catholic wing of the Church, he clearly must have had other qualities that outweighed the Bishop's Low Church preferences. The latter may, however, account for an odd comment he scribbled on Green's interview record card, which survives in the archives of the Museum of Army Chaplaincy.[10] Having noted that he had the necessary references and had been vetted by Scotland Yard, he added the curious comment 'very mincing manner: like Bristow!'[11] He had evidently found Green's general demeanour somewhat risible. It is easy to imagine how Green, a naturally reserved man, a little sensitive perhaps about his social status, might have appeared over-nice in his choice of words, afraid of saying the wrong thing.

Despite the Bishop's reservations, Green was found to be satisfactory and was offered a commission with the rank of TCF, 4th Class (the lowest grade). His pay was 10 shillings a day, with a penny-pinching allowance of £10 to buy his uniform and accoutrements, £40 less than the most junior infantry officer. Little or no training was provided at this stage of the war and newly appointed chaplains were simply thrown in at the deep end, there to sink or swim. Events now moved quickly. A buff envelope containing official notice of his appointment dropped through his letter box at 127 Dereham Road, Norwich, on Thursday 3 February. He had to be prepared to embark for overseas service in five days' time. With the weekend intervening there simply wasn't time to get his kit in order or to have the recommended inoculations. On a hurried trip to the Department's HQ in London the following morning Green requested a postponement of ten days, which was granted. He preached for the last time at St Barnabas' before going to war that Sunday, his sermon based on Psalm 121: 'The Lord shall keep thy going out and thy coming in'.[12] Official notice of his appointment was published in the *London Gazette* on St Valentine's Day, Monday 14 February 1916, the same day that he embarked for Flanders.

Green's first appointment was to a casualty clearing station (CCS). Few chaplains at this period were sent to the front line. Commanding officers in the field weren't quite sure they wanted them there or what purpose they would serve, and so the majority were sent to hospitals miles behind the lines. This led to a misconception, which grew after the war, that most chaplains were either 'shirkers' or hypocrites, urging soldiers to face dangers they chose not to face themselves, a myth popularised in novels and memoirs such as Robert Graves' *Goodbye to All That*. The hospital Green was sent to, designated CCS No. 22, was based at this time in a former Carmelite convent in Aire-sur-la-Lys in northern France. CCSs were mobile hospitals, third in a long chain of treatment centres set up to evacuate the wounded from the front. The injured were first treated at regimental aid posts then at advanced dressing stations. From there the more seriously wounded were moved by field ambulance to a CCS, from where those who survived and could be moved were transported to a stationary base hospital for further specialist treatment or recuperation, or back home to a hospital or sanatorium in 'Blighty'. Good lines of communication were essential and CCSs were usually situated near railway lines or canals. One problem was that most were too far from the fighting. During the Battle of Loos the previous year, the CCS at Aire was designated for abdominal wound cases. Casualties were taking two to three days to get there, and many died of shock or infection on route.[13]

An army chaplain's duties, apart from taking the compulsory Church Parade on Sunday mornings, were largely undefined. He could easily find himself cast in the role of general dogsbody. *The Times* correspondent writing in 1918 hit the nail on the head when he observed that an army chaplain 'is encouraged – nay, expected – to take on any job which is not specifically somebody else's'.[14] While at CCS 22 Green was called upon, amongst his numerous other semi-official duties, to act as censor, canteen manager and concert-party organiser. The first of these was a lesson in humility, as he sometimes found himself reading frank criticisms of him and his sermons written by soldiers who were unaware that the preacher on a Sunday was the censor on a Monday. It was also very time-consuming. The chaplain to CCS 21, the Revd Rupert Inglis, who was killed on the Somme in 1916, noted in his diary that he rather grudged spending four hours each day on this duty.[15] Green often had up to 250 letters a day from patients, medical orderlies and nurses to censor. Other work included visiting the wounded and writing letters for those unable to do so themselves. Inevitably, many of the patients succumbed to their wounds, and it was his job to collect their personal possessions, find the address of the next of kin (not always easy) and write them a consoling letter. He also had to conduct burial services, often a daily task. Amid all this sadness he was also expected to contribute to the raising of morale. Almost everything that made life slightly more tolerable – tinned

'Woodbine Willie' publicity photo
of the Revd Geoffrey Studdert Kennedy,
Green's almost exact contemporary

Popular postcard, reflecting
the importance placed on cigarettes in
keeping up the troops' morale

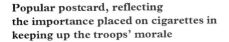

SMOKE CLOUDS (3).

When you're tired and weary, just jogging along,
And you have not a friend, and the whole world seems
        wrong.
Only gaze at the smoke clouds, and never despair,
For there's bound to be some silver lining somewhere.

fruit, jam, Camp coffee, biscuits, boot laces, razor blades, soap, reading
matter – was in short supply. Green soon became an expert scrounger and a
friend of all the nearby quartermasters. Above all else, the commodity most
in demand was cigarettes. Company commanders would frequently send
him notes, urging him to find some fags for their men, who could put up
with almost any hardship except going without a smoke. Green asked friends
back at St Barnabas' to start a 'Mag-Fag Fund', to buy or send cigarettes,
magazines and recent newspapers. After a while his efforts earned him the
nickname the 'Heigham Woodbine Willie', after the nickname of the famous
padre-poet, the Revd Geoffrey Studdert Kennedy, well-known for his
handing out of cigarettes in the trenches. Morale was also raised by concerts,
which Green helped to organise, putting on variety shows that drew on
whatever musical or theatrical talents the soldiers might possess.
Occasionally, a touring professional concert party put on a show, and during
Green's time at CCS 22, Lena Ashwell's famous troupe made a memorable
appearance.

In his first few weeks at CCS 22, with so many duties and obligations, Green seems, understandably, to have found it difficult to define what his real purpose was. Was he there to save souls or merely as a glorified entertainments officer cum undertaker? It was a dilemma most new chaplains found themselves pondering. The Chaplain-General's initial, less than flattering assessment was initially reinforced by the Assistant Chaplain-General to the 1st Army, the Revd Harry Blackburne, a blunt, former Boer War trooper, who seemed a little worried by Green's overly deferential manner.[16] On 8 March 1916 he took him to a CCS chaplains' conference in Lillers. Afterwards, he observed him at work at the hospital, noting in his diary: 'A good worker? ... anxious to do anything he can in and out of the hospital ... . Slightly apologetic manner.' Many chaplains were simply not up to the job, and it seems that Green's superiors had doubts whether the 'mincing curate' was tough enough. In time their doubts were entirely erased. In the harsh environment he now found himself in, with its Spartan living conditions and long hours of stressful work, Green developed into a confident and effective worker. Revisiting him five months later Blackburne noted that he was: 'Much liked by all at his CCS ... excellent work'. Six months later he would confidently assess him: 'A splendid Chaplain ... and unselfish'.[17] By this time Green had become something of a minor celebrity, having been mentioned in dispatches for 'distinguished and gallant services and devotion to duty',[18] and perhaps more importantly from a departmental point of view, having had his photograph

A youthful-looking Green in the uniform of an army chaplain, probably taken shortly after being commissioned in February 1916

16

published in the popular patriotic magazine, *The War Illustrated*, under the heading 'Chaplains Honoured for Gallantry in the Field'.[19] His photograph, probably taken soon after he had been commissioned, shows a slightly plump, smooth-faced young man, almost boyish in appearance, belying the fact that he was nearly 34 when it was taken. A photograph taken in 1919 (see frontispiece), just before he left the army, shows almost a different man, his face thinner, more worn, his gaze harder, more penetrating. Three years of war had done this.

Early in April 1916, CCS 22 was moved about twelve miles south-east to the town of Bruay, sixteen miles north-west of Arras. The French Army had handed over this sector of the front to the BEF in March. The British Army's Advising Consultant Surgeon, Sir Anthony Bowlby, had recommended moving CCS closer to the front in order to deal with the predicted heavy flow of wounded from the coming summer offensive. Bruay was, in his opinion, a step in the right direction, but still too small and too far from the fighting to be really effective. The trouble was that if they were too close to the front they could be shelled or even captured, as happened to Green's regimental aid post during the German's massive spring offensive in April 1918. In contrast with the ruined medieval splendour of Aire, Bruay was a grimy mining town, geared exclusively to keeping France's furnaces and railways supplied with coal. Green compared the slag heaps that dominated the surrounding landscape with 'Pyramids in the Egyptian desert', suggesting, perhaps consciously, the biblical symbolism of enslavement and exile this comparison implied. The hospital buildings – mainly just huts and tents – were situated right beside the railway line, handy for transporting the wounded, though the hiss and clank of the trains constantly interrupted Green's services and his sleep. Nevertheless, he decided to be stoical. Thinking perhaps of the punctilious Chaplain-General, Green wryly commented that 'Not being a Bishop, I am not perturbed by such untoward noises'.

Apart from a few days' leave in October, spent back in Norwich, Green remained at Bruay until early December. This was the period on the Western Front dominated by Verdun and the Somme, the most costly battles in terms of human life waged to that date. His letters written in July, August and September are almost entirely taken up with stories of individuals he had met on the wards or at a nearby Royal Flying Corps (RFC) airbase. Although Green or the censor suppressed their names, it is just possible to identify some of the men he met. He describes, for example, meeting a corporal, a professional footballer in civilian life, whose leg had been smashed. He knows that he will never play football again. After ten days he died. This man was almost certainly Corporal Albert Victor Butler, who died of wounds at Bruay on 13 May 1916. He had been in the 17th Battalion, Middlesex Regiment, a 'pals' unit, known as the 1st Footballers' Battalion because of the large number of professional footballers in its ranks.

During much of the spring and summer, RFC Squadron No. 18 was stationed at Bruay and so became part of Green's 'parish'. By an odd coincidence it had been stationed at Mousehold Heath[20] near Norwich the previous autumn, so it is just possible Green already knew some of the personnel; at the very least they would have had a great many local matters in common to talk about, such as the execution of the Norfolk nurse, Edith Cavell. In a letter written in September 1916 Green tells the story of a RFC officer he said he knew very well, an observer, killed in action in a dogfight. Official records show that this was almost certainly 2nd Lieutenant James Mitchell, an Irish-Canadian officer, aged 34, the same age as Green. His death occurred on a photo-reconnaissance patrol on 26 April 1916 when his two-man FE2b biplane was attacked by a Fokker. The pilot, who sat behind the observer, was uninjured and managed to get the badly damaged aircraft down safely. It was then that Mitchell was found to have been shot through the head. Green helped bury him in Bruay military cemetery, situated on a hillside overlooking the airfield. In the same letter he mentions talking to two young officers 'rigged out for flight' late one evening. The next day he heard that their plane had been forced to land in no man's land; both men had been killed and their aircraft destroyed by British artillery so as not to fall into the enemy's hands. The incident he relates was almost certainly one that occurred on the night of 15/16 July 1916, when a FE2b of No. 18 Squadron was sent up on a night bombing mission over the Somme battlefield. At about 1 a.m. it crash-landed near the German lines. What Green could not have known at the time was that although one of the crew, 2nd Lieutenant Harold Winstone Butterworth, a 21-year-old New Zealand officer, was killed, the other, Captain J. H. F. McEwan, survived although badly wounded and was taken prisoner. He was later handed over to see out the war in neutral Holland.

On 3 December 1916 Green was transferred from CCS 22 to the 56th Infantry Division. At first he was given two battalions to minister to, including the 1/4th London Regiment,[21] where he replaced the Revd R. Palmer MC, who had just been promoted to Senior Chaplain to the 24th Division. Then, sometime after Christmas, he was given responsibility for the spiritual well-being of the 1/4th Battalion alone. Green had a tough job on his hands. The 1/4th was made up of a thousand of some of the hardest drinking, hardest fighting men from the East End's meanest streets. Even the Battalion's official chronicler, Captain F. C. Grimwade, was forced to

18

describe its men as 'cheerful and optimistic, if blasphemous'.[22] The 1/4th Battalion, City of London Regiment (Royal Fusiliers) was a war-time Territorial unit formed during the national crisis in August 1914 from the ranks of the 4th Volunteer Battalion, Royal Fusiliers (originally known as the Tower Hamlet Rifles). After being posted to Malta for a few months in September 1914 to undertake garrison duties, the Battalion was attached to an Indian Army division and sent to Flanders, where it lost half its men during the 2nd Battle of Ypres in April 1915. In February 1916, after rebuilding its strength, the 1/4th found itself forming part of the 168th Brigade in the newly formed 56th (London) Division, along with three other London Territorial battalions: the Rangers, Kensingtons and London Scottish. In this formation it fought on the Somme, suffering particularly heavy casualties at the Battle of Gommecourt. After Green joined it, the 1/4th continued to serve on the Western Front almost continuously until it was disbanded soon after the Armistice, fighting at Arras, Passchendaele, Cambrai, Bapaume and the Sambre. Green was with it every step on the way and its soldiers became his family, friends and flock.

Life with an infantry battalion would prove to be considerably tougher than it had been at a CCS, though that had been a stern enough test in itself. Green now frequently found himself in the front line, sharing the same hardships and dangers as the men; living, sometimes for days on end, in underground dugouts that were constantly flooding and infested with rats. In April 1917 he wrote of the nightmarish experience of waking up to find a rat biting his nose. As a counter measure, abandoned farm cats were encouraged to take up residence and were ceremoniously handed on to the care of the next company to occupy that sector of line. The winter of 1916/17 was one of the coldest on record with temperatures reaching thirty degrees below freezing. Fires could not be lit for fear that the smoke would attract the enemy's attention. Even when not engaged in battle, there was a constant threat of being instantly atomised, burnt, eviscerated or buried alive by a shell or poisoned by gas. Enemy snipers and night-time bombing raids made life even more disagreeable.

When not in the trenches the men lived in rest billets a few miles behind the front line. These usually consisted of little more than wrecked farm buildings. They reminded Green of one of Captain Bruce Bairnsfather's famous cartoons in which a stoical, middle-aged infantry officer is depicted writing, 'Dear —. At present we are staying at a farm ...', while seated on an ammunition box outside a wrecked farmhouse, seemingly oblivious to the decomposing farm animals lying all around him. Bairnsfather's most famous cartoon caption, known and quoted all over the Western Front, was: 'If you knows of a better 'ole, go to it'. Darkly comic as it was, for many men who

19

Postcard of the Bairnsfather cartoon mentioned by Green

had experienced the front, such depictions of their daily life were closer to the truth than the sanitised or idealised artists' impressions reproduced in popular newspapers and magazines. The Christian writer, 2nd Lieutenant Donald Hankey, who died on the Somme in 1916, wrote: 'Men like Captain Bairnsfather have earned the right to mock, and in their mockery they often get closer to the portrayal of authentic heroism than do their more idealistic brethren'.[23] Green's war letters, while they do not mock, are similar in this sense, they seldom seek to preach, are rarely sentimental and do not flinch from describing the horrors of war, albeit within the bounds of taste and decency expected of a clergyman writing for a parish magazine. He avoided writing about things he hadn't experienced first-hand and tried to describe his experiences as honestly and in as straightforward a manner as possible. Above all else, his admiration and love for the ordinary soldier, whose hardships he shared, shines through every word he wrote. One might compare Green's letters with the more conventional writings of another chaplain of the 56th Division, the Revd Thomas Tiplady, who in a collection of 'fragments from the front' entitled *The Kitten in the Crater*, describes finding a kitten mewing in a bomb crater. For him the kitten is a symbol of innocence and hope in the midst of death and destruction. For Green a cat was a practical friend not a symbol. He even found it in his heart to forgive the ubiquitous rat, despite its nose-gnawing habits, writing how he once watched a mother rat carefully carry each of her offspring in her mouth to

20

safety after her nest was exposed by a shell. A story he tells simply without trying to turn it into a parable.

In March 1917, as the BEF geared itself up for the next big push, the 1/4th Battalion was moved from the Neuve Chapelle sector to the Arras sector, going into billets at Beaudricourt where it underwent a period of extensive training. Green was now allowed a week's leave and turned up unexpectedly one Tuesday evening at St Barnabas' Bible Class.[24] A party was held for him that week at which he gave a talk on life at the front. Much of his spare time was spent visiting families in the parish and collecting for the Mag-Fag Fund. War had by now transformed the social life of the parish. Almost every street had its own impromptu shrine, made of flowers, flags, ribbons, candles and lists of local soldiers and sailors, many now dead. Hardly a street had escaped bereave-

'The kitten in the crater', sentimental view of the army chaplains' work at the front

ment. With fewer men around as bread-winners, mothers and wives of men overseas formed their own self-help group named the Tipperary Club after the famous wartime song. Back in France, in early April, Green found the Battalion in new billets in Achicourt, a village that contained a largely undamaged Protestant chapel. Green immediately commandeered this for religious services. There had been some trouble with using France's more numerous Roman Catholic churches. Some French priests had refused to allow Protestant services to be held in them, while the Low Church Chaplain-General forbade any hint of ecumenicalism in the Department's

21

Contemporary illustration of a street war shrine

Women and children of Heigham during the war

official policy. Out in the battle zone matters were less clear-cut. On Easter Sunday, 8 April 1917, while Green was celebrating the Resurrection, Achicourt was shelled. The village held several batteries, shell dumps and ammunition wagons, some of which were hit and exploded. Several men who had been at one of Green's earlier services were killed. Two hours later the chapel itself was struck and Green wounded. A number of shell fragments remained embedded in his legs and were to cause him discomfort throughout the rest of his life. His wounds were sufficient for him to be listed among the Battalion's officer casualties as 'wounded at duty'.[25] The war was to have a debilitating effect on his health. He suffered from recurrent attacks of trench fever, a rickettsial bacterial infection contracted from the lice that infested clothing in the trenches. His health (and voice) was also not improved by being gassed during the closing weeks of the war.

Early the following morning, no doubt still in considerable pain, Green watched as waves of troops went over the top during a snowstorm along a fifteen-mile front. This was the commencement of the Battle of Arras, which was to last until late May and cost the BEF 150,000 casualties for little material gain. On that first day, known as the 1st Battle of the Scarpe, the 1/4th Battalion were held in reserve until the early afternoon, when they were sent onto a confused battlefield. While the Battalion's casualties this day were light, the Brigade as a whole lost over ninety men and hundreds more were wounded. Green spent the next sixteen hours tending the wounded at an advanced dressing station. The following day, in driving sleet and rain, still in pain from his leg wounds and having had no rest for two days, he went out onto the battlefield with a working party to carry out the gruesome job of trying to identify the dead, gather personal effects and give the frozen, mangled remains decent burial, one of the most awful tasks it befell an army chaplain to undertake. It was, he later wrote, 'a scene passing all description in its wretchedness and squalor'. One of Green's colleagues in the 168th Brigade, the Revd Julian Bickersteth, chaplain to the 12th Londons (Rangers), was engaged in similar work on this day. It was, he noted, the first battle in which they had been able to go out to 'pick up the wounded and dead in the old authorized fashion', [26] the reason being that they had gained enough ground the previous day for stretcher-bearers and burial parties (some manned by captured German soldiers) to move about at a safe distance from snipers. Usually the ground gained could only be measured in yards, and by this stage in the war the old niceties of chivalrous conduct in which the enemy was allowed to collect his dead and wounded unmolested had long been consigned to history.

The following six weeks were weary-making, as the Battalion consolidated the front line in bitterly cold weather before being moved hither

German prisoners helping to bring in the wounded

and thither around the French countryside, never spending more than a few days in any one billet before being shifted to bolster another sector of the front. On 17 May Green visited a soldiers' club, similar perhaps to the famous one known as Talbot House in Poperinghe near Ypres, which was the inspiration for Toc H after the war. Here he ran into a former colleague, the Revd Edward St George Schomberg, who had joined St Barnabas' as a curate at about the same time as Green but had left in October 1914. Schomberg, who was now vicar of Norton St Philip, Somerset, was an army chaplain in France during 1916 and 1917. Two days later, while moving to new billets at Berneville, Green had a further reminder of home when a number of 7th Battalion Norfolk Regiment soldiers from Heigham recognised and hailed him. On 20 May the exhausted troops of the 1/4th London Battalion were finally relieved for a period of three weeks rest and training. As it was a Sunday, a compulsory Church Parade for the entire Brigade was ordered, a rare event as so large a body of men out in the open presented a potential target for enemy aircraft directing long-range artillery. A description of the parade is recorded in the diary of the Revd Bickersteth. Standing on an army wagon, with a table covered in a Union Jack for an altar, Green took the service while Bickersteth preached. Over 2,000 men attended, which Bickersteth thought too large a congregation as many simply could not hear what was being said. Matters were not helped by the constant noise of artillery and of planes passing overhead. In a letter probably written in July 1917, but recounting events from this period, Green recalled being told by an army commander that the first requisite of a good sermon was brevity. It did not do to be standing still too long out in the open.

In early June, still blessedly out of the firing line, the whole Division held a sports day. A bicycle race between chaplains and doctors on old French boneshakers over rough ground was run, with Bickersteth winning. Whether or not as a consequence, a couple of months later he was promoted to Senior Chaplain to the 56th Division, so becoming Green's immediate superior. A week or so later the Battalion undertook another tour of duty before returning to billets in Achicourt in early July, a place of painful memories for Green, where he had been wounded by a shell almost three months earlier. The next day, fighting having now almost completely ceased around Arras, the Battalion was transported in trucks and London buses south across the old Somme battlefield to the Hébuterne area, a haunted place for the Battalion, where it had fought a bitter, ineffective and costly battle a year earlier, before Green's time. In a letter written a couple of months later, Green writes of the desolate landscape and ruined villages of the Somme. He describes in particular a shattered village partly hidden in a decimated wood, possibly Gommecourt, which the Battalion had failed to capture in July 1916, but was now in Allied hands, the garden of one obliterated house surreally blooming with roses.

Before long the Division was warned to be ready to move to a new sector, back into Flanders near the Belgian town of Ypres. A new offensive was in preparation, a monument to human folly and misery that become known as Passchendaele. On 16 August 1917, during a badly planned attack along the Menin Road at a place known as Inverness Copse, the 1/4th Battalion suffered one of the worst days in its history, losing about sixty killed and hundreds wounded or missing. Green makes no mention of the catastrophe in his letters. The censor in any case would not have allowed it. The Revd Bickersteth, who was now senior divisional chaplain, noted in his diary that during the Ypres campaign he and his chaplains wrote between three and four thousand letters to relatives of the dead and wounded. A week or so after the bloody disaster at Inverness Copse, Green was back in Norwich on leave, a bout of trench fever prolonging his stay to ten days. Despite feeling ill, he preached on the subject of the war at St Barnabas' on successive Sundays as well as giving a talk on his recent experiences to a crowded gathering in the church hall.[27] A concert to raise funds for the Mag-Fag Fund was also held. Writing of the visit in the parish magazine, the vicar noted that: 'He always brings the message of the cheerful endurance of all ranks in the face of the indescribable horrors of war, and makes us ashamed of our easy-going lives and slackness in the duty of prayer'.[28] The

25

latter was something that clearly worried Green and to which he would return in a number of his letters.

Green returned to France on 5 September, writing of the experience with remarkable frankness in his next letter: 'Returning from leave is a very trying time. For the more you see of war the less you like it, and when you return from leave you return to trenches and shells, desolation and nasty smells.' Finding that the 56th Division had moved in his absence to the Bapaume area, he had to spend a few days at 'a vast base camp' awaiting transport. The camp was almost certainly that at Etaples. His stay there coincided with the very weekend when serious disturbances broke out after British and Australian troops were goaded into rioting by the harsh conditions and often humiliating treatment they had had to endure there at the hands of the camp's training instructors, known derisively as 'canaries', many of whom, to the disgust of the battle-wearied troops they were persecuting, had never even been to the front. The riot, later known as the 'Bull-Ring Mutiny', was hushed up for many years, and although Green must have been aware of it, as he was actually there the day it broke out, he could not have alluded to it in his letters without it being censored and himself reprimanded. There is perhaps just a hint that he may have had some sympathy for the rioters' grievances in the letter he wrote on 5 October, which is critical of the dirty, draughty horse boxes, luggage wagons and filthy, broken-down railway carriages that men and junior officers had to travel in for long periods of time on excruciatingly slow-moving trains. He also remarked in the same letter that the men who do the fighting deserved more leave than those who didn't. What he could not say outright was that, as every Tommy knew, staff officers travelled in comparative luxury and had more frequent and longer periods of leave, a cause of simmering resentment.

When he finally rejoined his battalion he found it entrenched at the wrecked hamlet of Lagnicourt, facing the heavily fortified Hindenburg line, where the Germans had strategically withdrawn earlier in the year. The next two months were relatively quiet ones spent consolidating the line, with few casualties and no major engagements. There was talk of peace in the air. In July the Reichstag had passed a resolution demanding that the German Supreme Command negotiate a peace settlement 'without annexations or indemnities', meaning, in effect, a return to the pre-war status quo without reparations or war-guilt. Amid a debate in Britain and America about whether or not to pursue a cessation of hostilities by diplomatic means, Lieutenant Siegfried Sassoon issued his famous anti-war statement, leading to questions being asked in the House of Commons. For Green the only peace worth having now was a victorious peace. It is clear from his letters that while he loathed the war, he was not a pacifist. Although, like every

26

other soldier in the trenches, he longed for an end to the war, he believed that the enemy had to be beaten to its knees and punished for the wrongs it had done, 'whatever the cost'. It is unlikely, however, that he would have gone as far as the editor of the *Modern Churchman*, H. D. A. Major, who wrote in August 1917: 'If the only way to protect adequately an English babe is to kill a German babe, then it is the duty of our authorities, however repugnant, to do it'.[29]

Green began now to express in his parish letters the feeling held by many at the front, including it seems himself, that many of those safely at home had forgotten them or made light of their sacrifices. Like many clergymen he had hoped that the war would bring about a resurgence in church-going and prayer. In 1916 he had enthusiastically supported the National Mission of Repentance and Hope, a Church of England initiative to create national moral rearmament. Its work had proved largely ineffectual. He was disappointed to find on his leave that the pubs, cinemas and musical halls were fuller than ever while many churches stood empty. For Green, prayers for the soldiers at the front showed that the people at home still cared about them, and knowing that the people back home still cared was one of the things that helped get them through their hardships. It was one of the few occasions when Green used his war-time parish letters to preach and instruct his congregation back home, so strong were his feelings on this issue.

November 1917 arrived and the stalemate along the Hindenburg line continued. Preparations were being made for another winter in the line. The immediate problem, however, was the rain, or more particularly the mud it caused. Mud was everywhere, reminding Green of something he was reading in a book by a French soldier for whom mud was one of the worst horrors of the war. This was almost certainly Henri Barbusse's *Le Feu*, a classic of Great War literature first translated and published in English in 1917 with the title *Under Fire*. The final chapter would not have made comfortable reading for a parson, a group of men whom Barbusse classed with financiers, speculators and reactionary politicians as enemies of human progress. Green makes no mention of Barbusse's politics, but he disagreed with him about the mud. It was bad, but there were worse horrors, much worse.

Meanwhile, the shivering, mud-caked troops in the front line were beginning to think that campaigning had been postponed for the winter. They were wrong. On 20 November the 1st Battle of Cambrai was launched. It had been planned in utmost secrecy. For the first time, tanks were used on the first day to open the way through the thick barbed-wire entanglements without the usual preliminary bombardment, which had been so ineffective in the past at cutting the wire and so effective in alerting the enemy's machine gunners that a new attack across no man's land was on the way. The element of surprise and the tank-made paths through the wire brought about early successes, which typically the senior commanders failed to follow up. What had been envisaged as an open-ground fight turned into an almost subterranean struggle. The 1/4th Battalion were held back until the 23rd. The Germans, entrenched near the village of Moeuvres in their sector of the line, had by now fallen back to their second line of defence, so much of the fighting was along the communication trenches that joined their first and second trench systems. These had been barricaded by 'blocks' by both sides. The fighting that took place in these narrow, confined spaces was intense and often hand to hand. The trenches behind the barricades, which were being continuously shelled and counter-attacked, were soon crowded with the wounded, whom it was too dangerous to move. The Battalion was finally relieved by the Kensingtons on the 26th. Green's work during these terrible three days was singled out for special praise in the Battalion's official history:

> The Padre, S. F. Leighton Green, did splendid work throughout, being always about the Hindenburg lines and going up to the advanced blocks. At night he was constantly visiting and helping the casualties and administering the last rites to those who had fallen.[30]

The Church of England did not have an officially sanctioned ritual for the dying, such as the Roman Catholic Church's sacrament of extreme unction, though some Anglican clergy did administer unction to the dying. The Chaplain-General, however, actively discouraged its use. Mention of his administering the last rites may mean that Green, an Anglo-Catholic, was one of the few Anglican chaplains to carry the reserved sacrament and unction. However, 'last rites' here may simply mean the burial service. In a parish letter Green wrote after the war he recalled the aftermath of battle:

> I remember several nights at Cambrai in November, 1917, I took out a burial party to clear the battlefield, and we made a little cemetery behind the Hindenburg line. On the last night, after the last broken, battered body had been laid to rest and the words of faith and commendation had been said, the sergeant in charge of the party turned to me as we were filling in the trench: 'Let us hope,' he said, ' that some good will come out of this — business.'[31]

It takes little imagination to fill in the blank.

The Battalion spent the remainder of the month holding the front line against counter-attacks. On 1 December they were relieved and moved to

An army chaplain conducting a burial service in the field

rest billets at Simencourt for a few days before going into the line again for a long tour of duty in the trenches near Oppy. On Sunday 16 December, while in rest billets at Ecurie, Green officiated at a Church Parade at which the 56th Division's CO, Major-General Dudgeon, presented gallantry medal ribbons to the men and NCOs who had been awarded DCMs and MMs for their work at Cambrai. Christmas was spent in the trenches, where, as Green noted, 'there was anything but "peace on earth"'. On Christmas Day a shell killed 2nd Lieutenant Edwin Stuckey, a 20-year-old officer attached from the 17th Londons who had helped save the day during a critical moment in the trench fighting at Cambrai. At the end of month the Battalion withdrew to billets at St Aubin where it combined its postponed regimental Christmas dinner with New Year's celebrations. Green wrote that everyone hoped that next Christmas would be spent at home, though a pessimist among them murmured, 'What 'opes!'

Early in January 1918 the Battalion moved to new billets at Monchy Breton, some twenty miles behind the front line. Here it spent its first long period of rest for six months. It was almost a holiday for the men, although, as Green noted, their accommodation in the local farm buildings was far from luxurious. The village itself was undamaged, a rare sight, and the

29

enemy's guns only a distant flash and rumble on the horizon. Green now came back to Norwich on leave, the first time he had been back since September. He stayed for a little over a week and preached on the war at St Barnabas' on successive Sundays, the second of which coincided with a service to mark the twelfth anniversary of the church's consecration.[32] It was a time of anniversary for himself too. He was about to complete two years' service as an army chaplain, and had already signed up for a further year's service. It was a time to take stock.

The first letter he wrote on return to France in February seems to mark a subtle shift in Green's emotional attachments. While St Barnabas' is still very much in his thoughts, there is a hint that he had begun to feel detached from his former life and to see the Battalion as his real congregation. He wrote now to the vicar suggesting that someone else, perhaps one of the men serving in Palestine, take over the job of writing the monthly letters. His request was refused and so he dutifully continued. It is noticeable, however, that his letters now became shorter, while in May, for the first time in over two years, he missed his deadline.

While he was on leave his front-line congregation had grown and there were many new members for him to get to know. On 13 February, Ash Wednesday, the 56th Division was visited by the Deputy Chaplain-General, the Right Revd Llewellyn Gwynne, Bishop of Khartoum, who confirmed forty soldiers in a little wooden chapel dedicated to St Stephen, the first Christian martyr. The chapel, which had been built by the Division's sappers, was located in the divisional reserve camp at Roclincourt where the 1/4th Battalion were currently in rest billets after another tour of duty in the trenches near Oppy. Bishop Gwynne was a much more approachable character than the Chaplain-General, Bishop Taylor Smith, and generally well thought of both as an administrator and as a spiritual guide. Unlike the Chaplain-General, who spent most of his time behind a desk in London, Bishop Gwynne was permanently based in France. His views were ecumenical and he encouraged and supported chaplains from all religious persuasions. He had also instituted a much-needed chaplains' training college in St Omer. An anecdote told by Bishop Gwynne to Brigadier-General Reginald Kentish, with whom he was sharing a staff car on his way from St Omer to Amiens in June 1917, might very well be about Green. Asked by Gwynne what he thought of chaplains, General Kentish had replied that: 'they were either men of the world and very human, and so got on splendidly with the troops, or else they were neither the one nor the other, cut very little ice, and found their task a very difficult one'. Bishop Gwynne then told him about a chaplain of the former sort, attached to a London Regiment, who always lived in the front line whenever the battalion went into the trenches rather than remaining with the HQ some way back. He had his own dugout with a sign saying 'The Vicarage'. One day a cockney soldier new to the trench came across the sign and remarked to his comrade, 'Gorblimey, Bill! who'd 'ave fought of seein' the bloody vicarage in the front line?' At this the padre popped his head out from behind the blanket covering the entrance and replied, 'Yes! And who'd have thought of seeing the bloody vicar too?'[33]

On 21 March 1918 the long-expected German spring offensive known as the *Kaiserschlacht* or Kaiser's Battle began. The full brunt of the onslaught did not fall on the 1/4th Battalion's sector of the line near Oppy until a week later. The intervening period, which coincided with Passion Week, was an anxious time with furious activity to get the defences in order. Consequently there was little time for the men to attend religious services and, in any case, the Battalion's little improvised chapel, St Stephen's, had been badly damaged by shrapnel and shell blast. Even the harmonium's bellows were punctured, showing just how close the on-coming battle was getting. In the early hours of the 28th a report came in that the enemy had been seen moving up their trenches in large numbers. At this time, Green was at the Battalion's forward command HQ in 'Ouse Alley' trench, which almost immediately came under shell fire, including gas. A few hours later an SOS signal came in to HQ that the enemy's infantry attack had begun. At this, the Battalion's CO, Lieutenant-Colonel Allan Marchment, sent his HQ Company to reinforce the outlying defences, keeping with him just a handful of signallers and staff and 'Padre Green to create a calm atmosphere'.[34] His calming presence would soon be needed, for half an hour later the HQ was shelled again and the Battalion's Works officer, Lieutenant Lorden, badly wounded. To make matters worse the regimental aid post with all of its wounded and medical staff, including the chief medical officer, Captain Maloney, was captured. The Battalion was finally relieved in the evening, having just about held the line but having lost in the process nineteen killed, forty-five wounded and over 170 missing, many probably by now prisoners of war. The exhausted survivors marched through the night to billets at Mont St Eloy, arriving, in Green's words, 'a weary and depleted crowd'. Here, on Sunday 31 March, Green celebrated his second Easter with the 1/4th Battalion; neither had been exactly the happy occasion he had prayed for.

In early April the Battalion received drafts of new troops to rebuild its strength. Some, as Green noted, were veterans with wound stripes on their sleeves, some just lads of 19, fresh from home and keen to do their bit. The character of the Battalion was changing. Where once it had been almost exclusively manned by East Enders, now the camp was transformed into 'a mild imitation of the Tower of Babel' with accents from London, Kent, Surrey, Berkshire, Yorkshire, Cheshire, Lancashire, Wiltshire, Scotland and south Wales. In addition, the men were no longer all drawn from the Territorials, but included men, especially experienced NCOs, from Regular battalions as well. All this meant hard work for the padre, getting to know all the new faces.

On the 9 April the Germans launched the second phase of their spring offensive, the Lys Offensive. On the 11th, Field Marshall Haig issued his famous 'to the last man' order. This was a time of acute crisis when the outcome of the war was balanced on a knife-edge. In a letter written four days later, Green restated his belief in the rightness of the cause they were fighting for in words that are almost a paraphrase of Haig's order:

> We are fighting for our homes, for liberty and righteousness in the world, for the safety and welfare of generations yet unborn. In such a cause we should be willing to fight and to suffer, and if need be to die.[35]

He was particularly appalled by stories reaching him from home that during Holy Week, at this time of supreme national crisis, the music halls were crowded and the churches nearly empty, unaware perhaps that censorship was keeping the true state of affairs on the Western Front from the people.

After a bad few weeks the crisis passed, and by the end of April the Germans' spring offensive seemed to have exhausted itself. American troops were now flooding into France and there was a feeling that it was only a matter of time before Germany was defeated. Nevertheless, the next few months were an anxious time, characterised by Green as one of 'constant watchfulness', every moment expecting another surprise attack, which thankfully never came. In this state of heightened anxiety and expectation, it was important to maintain morale and 'buck things up'. An important element in morale was the canteen, which he was tireless in his efforts to supply with palatable food and cigarettes. Another was the Battalion orchestra, which had been formed by the quartermaster, Lieutenant Faulkner, in Monchy Breton back in January. Green encouraged it and helped organise divisional concert parties known as the Bow Bells, alluding to the Division's cockney origins. The band, comprising four violins, two cellos and assorted brass, woodwind, percussion and a portable harmonium, also became Green's church orchestra, playing the hymns and voluntaries at services when the Battalion was out of the line. After the war, the harmonium, painted with all the names of the French and Belgian towns and villages the band had performed in, was presented to Green for use at St Barnabas'.

In August the tide had turned sufficiently in the Allies' favour for them to launch their own offensive. The 1/4th Battalion had spent the preceding three months in and around Arras, rebuilding its strength, defending the front line and taking part in the occasional trench raid. On 21 August orders came for it to march south towards Bapaume. The Division had just been hastily transferred from XVII to VI Corps and communications had broken down, so that nobody seemed sure where exactly they were going or how to get there. This was unfamiliar territory and even some of the guides sent to lead them lost their way. HQ Company got hopelessly lost and did not turn up until long after the battle had commenced. Green, who was with them, thought that they had been taken for a long walk around the town of Albert, about ten miles south-west of where they should have been. When they finally turned up, the battle was already under way. Lieutenant-Colonel Marchment, without his HQ Company, was trying to conduct the battle and guard 200 German prisoners with just five staff. Green and the Battalion's new medical officer, Captain E. Woodyeat, a retired naval surgeon, who had also got lost, went immediately to tend the wounded. By 29 August the Division was fighting inside the Hindenburg line and temporarily captured Bullecourt. That night the 1/4th Battalion camped in the enemy's former trenches, where it was heavily bombed. It was probably here that Green took a whiff of gas, perhaps while resting without his mask on. At this stage of the war the German were mainly using mustard gas, not as instantly fatal as chlorine but just as insidious; almost odourless it clung to uniforms and skin and contaminated the ground, causing blisters, blindness and vomiting.

On Sunday 15 September, presumably after a couple of weeks' recuperation, Green was on leave in Norwich, which he hadn't visited for six months.[36] Despite his voice having been affected by the gas, he gave an account of the last critical eight months in France. Pressed for his opinion on when the war would end, he refused to comment but said he was encouraged by the hopefulness of the situation. A week later he was back in France, at Feuchy, with his beloved battalion, camped near a wrecked railway line in pits and shell holes covered by sheets of tarpaulin during a spell of wet and windy weather. Despite the primitive conditions, the absence of the enemy saw a return to some of the decorous ceremonies of more peaceful times. At 7.30 each evening the Battalion bugler would sound 'Dress for Mess' and half-an-hour later the officers would emerge from their holes in the ground smartly dressed to partake of a five-course dinner. Green himself had to dress for dinner in the formal wear of an army chaplain of the

Victorian era, which included black-cloth knee-breeches, black silk stockings and patent leather black shoes with plain silver buckles.

Following its victory at Bapaume, the BEF was beginning to push into territory that had been in German hands since 1914. Refugees from the French and Belgian villages in front of the advancing Allies streamed back through their lines, escaping the oncoming battle. On 27 September the 1/4th Battalion took part in the 2nd Battle of Cambrai, crossing the Hindenburg line at the Canal du Nord. Some of the destruction Green witnessed here, carried out by the retreating German forces, seemed to him quite pointless and vindictive, such as the vandalised churches and the home of a curé Green visited, his furniture and books smashed and trampled. He also inspected the German's hastily abandoned hospitals and accompanying cemeteries with their graves of German and British soldiers. On 15 October the Battalion went into rest billets in Arras. Here Green and his battle-hardened comrades encountered more refugees, heard their terrible stories

Arras in ruins, as witnessed by Green in 1918

and visited children in the hospital, some dying of gas poisoning, giving up a portion of their rations to the starving civilians. Their stay here, however, wasn't all sad. On 21 October the Battalion provided the guard of honour for a visiting VIP, whom no one recognised but who turned out to be the President of France, Raymond Poincaré. Ten days later they were bussed to billets in the village of Douchy near Denain, which had been in enemy hands only eight days before. Here on 1 November, All Saints' Day, Green attended a service in a Roman Catholic church in which locals and soldiers joined together to give thanksgiving – the old religious divisions temporarily forgotten in the joy of liberation.

The war, however, was not yet over. The next day the Battalion began marching towards the Belgian border, losing four men killed and fourteen wounded by shell fire when passing through the village of Famars. On the morning of 4 November, the Battalion found itself in front of the enemy-occupied village of Sebourquiaux on the west bank of the Aunelle valley. Their objective lay across exposed, steeply undulating terrain. Luckily their advance was covered by an early morning mist. However, on entering the outskirts of the village they came under intense bombardment and were trapped here for several hours until a flanking manoeuvre drove off the occupying Germans. Having taken the village, the Battalion became trapped once again, unable to advance up the steep slope to the east of the village that formed the crest of the west side of the valley. Sebourquiaux was bombarded all day until not a building was left standing. It was here that Green won a bar to his Military Cross. It is not recorded for what specific action he won his first MC, which was gazetted on 1 January 1919. However, a full citation for his second MC, gazetted on 2 April 1919, was published in the *London Gazette* on 9 December 1919, over a year after the event it described:

> For conspicuous gallantry and devotion to duty at Sebourquiaux on 4th November 1918. During the advance he attended to the wounded, frequently under heavy fire. He went forward and stayed for over an hour with a badly wounded signaller lying out in the open under shell fire, until the stretcher-bearers could fetch him away.[37]

On 5 November the 1/4th London Battalion entered Belgium and continued pursuing the retreating Germans towards the Grand Honelle River, where it fought its last battle of the war on the 6th, losing thirteen men killed and fifty-seven wounded or missing. Under cold, driving rain, through liberated villages and towns where crowds flocked to cheer them, the Battalion marched on for mile after mile, arriving at the Belgian village of Sars-la-Bruyère on the 10th. Here on the following morning they received a telegram from Brigade HQ with news that hostilities would cease at 11 a.m. The Battalion diary notes: 'The news had an unexpected effect on the troops: everybody appeared to be too dazed to make any demonstration. Men were much less cheerful than they had been for days.'[38] Green observed that they were all dead tired and too worn out to celebrate at once, but greatly relieved that the war was finally over.

There had been talk of the Battalion going into Germany with the occupying Army of the Rhine, but this had come to nothing. The Battalion remained in the Mons area, where the first major battle of the war had been fought over four years earlier. Few men now left in the Division remembered it, and of the 1,016 officers and men of the 1/4th Battalion who sailed for Malta in September 1914, only thirty now remained in the Battalion. One of the most noteworthy survivors was Flossie, the Battalion dog, a small, brown Pomeranian, which had raised several litters of puppies on the way. On 27 November, after a triumphal march through Mons, the Battalion was billeted at Villers-sire-Nicole near Maubeuge. The next Christmas at home that everyone had wished for in 1917 hadn't come true, but the next best thing, Christmas at peace, had miraculously occurred. Here Green oversaw the construction of the last of the Battalion's little improvised chapels, and it was here that he said his goodbyes to his comrades of the last two years.

Back in St Barnabas' in December, the vicar wrote of the spontaneous outburst of joy that greeted the news of peace: 'November 11, the Feast of St Martin, the soldier-saint of France, will be long remembered by all, when at 11 a.m. flags and bunting appeared as if by magic in the streets, the sirens sounded "all clear," and bells rang joyfully the long-expected peace. ... Everybody is now asking "When will Mr Green be home?"'[39] It seems clear, however, that he didn't really want to go just yet and would have preferred to remain with his battalion until it was demobbed as a whole. In his last letter written from Flanders, Green remarks that someone had written to him to say that now that he had nothing much to do he might as well come home. Far from having nothing much to do, he related with evident pride that he was currently chaplain to 4,000 men scattered over many square miles and had eight Church Parades to manage each Sunday (which means he was probably covering the whole Brigade). He also had a weekly Bible class, a guild of communicants, a confirmation class, a library, a canteen, a magazine, a debating society, and Latin lessons to conduct. It was presumably the Revd Lanchester who was pulling strings to get him home early. In the parish magazine the vicar noted that: 'the Army authorities were loath to let him go' and his demob was the result of 'strenuous efforts'.[40] The London Regiment's official history records the feelings of the 1/4th Battalion for their departing padre:

> Among the first to leave was the padre, Rev. S. F. Leighton Green, M.C., who had served continuously with the Battalion since December 1916. The padre left on the 13th February 1919, and his departure was felt most keenly by every officer and man in the Battalion. His constant selfless devotion to duty and his kindly

personality had made him a true friend to one and all, and the example of his simple life and magnificent courage in action had been a real inspiration to all – and that included the whole Battalion – who had been brought into personal contact with him.[41]

The Revd Blackburne, who had been somewhat unsure of Green's suitability for the job back in March 1916, wrote on completion of his service: 'I cannot speak too highly of the bravery and devotion to duty of this chaplain. Wherever he has been he has been admired and respected.'[42]

Green's return to Civvy Street was rapid and no doubt disorientating. His temporary commission ended on the day he left the Battalion. Six days later his army pay was stopped. A week after that he was no longer entitled to wear his uniform, though he was later appointed an Honorary Chaplain to the Forces. He now threw himself into his pastoral work with feverish intensity. Much of the parish, like virtually every other parish in the land, was itself quite literally feverish with the great influenza pandemic, which eventually killed more people than the war. He agreed, reluctantly, having been asked by 'the competent authority' (presumably the vicar), to continue writing his monthly letters for the parish magazine until the end of the year. He used them to talk to his congregation, particularly the ex-servicemen, about ways in which they might continue the spirit of comradeship they had experienced in the war. He tried to visit all of the men returning from active service and did what he could to help them readjust to civilian life while valuing their service and honouring the memory of those of their comrades who would never return. In this he was close to the aims of such organisations as Toc H, founded by two former army chaplains[43] and, later, the British Legion, a forerunner of which, the Federation of Discharged and Demobilised Soldiers and Sailors, was active in the parish. He revived the pre-war Men's Club, where local working-class men could enjoy recreational, teetotal activities, such as whist and billiards, over a pipe or two of tobacco, and the Men's Bible Class, an educational group where there were discussions, not just of religious but also of topical and historical subjects. He also began a Men's Service, with prayers, hymns and talks on inspirational subjects, which he delivered extempore from the chancel steps rather than from the pulpit. In July 1919 he organised a war exhibition in the church hall, where local ex-servicemen brought along souvenirs of their time in the forces, including even some weapons. The parish's war dead were commemorated in a memorial service and by a new stained-glass east window. A war shrine, partly paid for by Green, containing the names and regiments of those from the parish who had died on active service, was constructed inside the church as a permanent version of the informal street

**St Barnabas' Roll of Honour, commemorating the heaviest casualties
suffered by any parish in Norwich**

shrines with flags and flowers that had been a striking feature of the parish
during the war.

All this work, taken without any holiday, eventually took its toll on his
health. In June 1920, the vicar announced that: 'owing to a breakdown due
to the strain of the war, Mr Green has been ordered a prolonged rest and
will be away for several weeks'.[44] In fact he didn't return until August.
Whether his breakdown was mental as well as physical is not known, though
it seems probable given the length of his absence and the immense stress that
he had been under for the past few years. As he approached the end of his
thirties he seems to have come to the decision that he needed to move on
and shepherd his own flock, as he had done with his beloved battalion in the
war. In January 1921 he announced to a shocked Parochial Church Council
that he had been offered and had accepted the living of All Saints,
Mundesley.

Mundesley was perhaps a strange choice.[45] Given his exemplary war
record and his standing in the Anglo-Catholic community one might have
expected him to move to one of the larger Anglo-Catholic churches in
London or Oxford. Instead he went to a small seaside resort, still busy with
holiday-makers in the summer season but years past its Edwardian heyday.

All Saints, Mundesley, as Green would have known it

The restored interior of All Saints, which Green helped to complete. Note the parish war memorial plaque to the left of the chancel arch

The previous incumbent, the Revd Tegg Harvey, who had retired on health grounds in 1920, had rebuilt the medieval parish church of All Saints almost single-handed between 1903 and 1914, restoring what had been a partial ruin since the eighteenth century. It was left to Green to complete the work of furnishing the interior. He devoted much of his energy to this task, including the installation of a new east window. He also saw the need and helped raise funds for the building of some public rooms outside the church's ancient fabric, where parishioners could meet and hold social functions and public meetings. The large old rectory was sold in 1924 and he lived in a smaller house, St Winifred's. He also became involved in local organisations outside the Church: he was president of the local branch of the British Legion, sat on the board of the local hospital and helped run the Sea Scouts. He seems to have found happiness doing good works in a quiet place and he was loved by all who knew him.

The end when it came was swift and unexpected. Like Solomon Grundy in the old nursery rhyme, he was well on the Sunday, taken ill on the Monday, was worse on the Tuesday and died on the Wednesday. On 26 May 1929 he celebrated Trinity Sunday in All Saints, said mass the following morning and fell ill later that day. As his condition rapidly deteriorated he was rushed to a nursing home in Newmarket Road in Norwich and had his appendix removed on Tuesday. He died the following day, 29 May 1929, aged 47, his brother Arthur at his bedside. His death certificate gave the cause of death as pneumonia and gangrenous appendicitis, lingering symptoms perhaps of the debilitating effects of the war, not least the mustard gas he had inhaled in 1918.

Among the many obituaries that appeared in the local press, one described an almost Father Brown-like character: 'There was something of the friendly abbé about his manner and appearance. Strangers to Mundesley in the summer months were frequently surprised by the sight of this genial cleric, wearing biretta, or broad-rimmed hat, and cassock, making his way to the church or a pastoral call'.[46] A few months after his death his old task master, the Revd Lanchester, printed an edited selection of his war-time letters under the title *The Happy Padre*, echoing that impression of geniality he had always exuded. Priced at one shilling, it had a purely local sale and soon became out of print. By an odd coincidence Green's death occurred only twelve weeks after that of his almost exact contemporary and fellow army chaplain, the Revd Geoffrey Studdert Kennedy, 'Woodbine Willie', whose nickname still lives in the national consciousness. By contrast Green, the 'Heigham Woodbine Willie', has been almost completely forgotten. Even his grave in Mundesley churchyard has no marker.[47] It is hoped that what earthly fame he may now have will rest on the republication of his letters, dutifully and lovingly written month by month amid the grim desolation of the Western Front a long, long lifetime ago.

Studio portrait of Green, probably taken shortly before leaving St Barnabas' in 1921

The Letters

Letter 1

Somewhere in Flanders
[written at CCS 22, Aire, Pas de Calais, France]
St. Patrick's Day [Friday 17 March 1916]

Dear People,

My first letter to you arrived too late for the February Magazine, but the contents, I understand, have been communicated to you all.[48] In that letter I described the work of a Chaplain at a casualty clearing station. The work is one of great human interest. There are sick and wounded men in the station from all branches of the Services – Sappers, Gunners, Flying Corps, Cavalry, and in many ways the most wonderful of all, the Infantry of the Line. Many of them have come here within a few hours of leaving the trenches. The great difficulty of a Chaplain's work is that these soldiers only remain for a few days at the most, and then they return to duty or are sent away to a General Hospital at the Base.

Aire-sur-la-Lys, Green's first posting

42

There is a constantly changing population. The only cases not quickly removed are those of men who are so critically ill or dangerously wounded that it is inadvisable to move them. Some of these cases gradually improve till they are well enough to go elsewhere by hospital train or by hospital barge. The others terminate fatally. These men come here to die. Of your charity, remember such in your prayers

In this letter I want to tell you something about the station. In some respects its situation is good. We are housed in a Convent from which the Carmelite nuns were expelled some years ago. After many vicissitudes the buildings were used as a House of Retreat and then some twelve months ago they were rented by the British Government to house this Casualty Clearing Station. The buildings form a square, and the inner sides of the square enclose a garden, in the centre of which stands a beautiful statue of Our Lady and the Holy Child. An enclosed cloister runs round the whole square. The character of the buildings make necessary a large number of small wards, for few rooms are capable of taking more than ten patients. There is indeed one larger ward with two dozen patients – it is the dismantled Chapel. Over the cloisters the staff of the Station have their rooms. My room is a small cell. When I entered it for the first time there was one, and only one, article of furniture – a Crucifix. Under that Crucifix there is now a stretcher on tressels – my bed.[49] My kit supplied the rest. What more could a man want? It is luxury. In another cell I have been able to arrange a small chapel, and there on Sundays and other Holy Days and on Thursday each week at 7.30 a.m., the Holy Eucharist is offered.

So much for the buildings. I will now tell you about the staff. This Station is commanded by an officer of the R.A.M.C. [Royal Army Medical Corps], and he is assisted by seven doctors and a dentist. The latter is, I believe, one of the hardest worked men out here. He is visited by soldiers with the toothache from miles around. He most certainly is doing his "bit." There is also a quartermaster, whose chief business in life appears to be to accumulate all the stores he can lay hands on, and he does this with great energy. Last, but not least, there are the three padres – the Roman Catholic Chaplain, the Presbyterian Chaplain, and myself. The two former are capital fellows. Modesty forbids my saying anything about the third.

We often heard at home of the great work of the R.A.M.C, at the Front.[50] What we heard was in no way exaggerated. The devotion, care and skill of the doctors here are beyond all praise. Many of them have come out at great sacrifice to themselves from a financial point of view, and their great achievements in medical and surgical science will make a great chapter in the history of the War. Their work is well backed up by the Army Nursing Sisters and eighty men of the R.A.M.C. It is wonderful what a tender-

43

hearted night attendant a man who less than twelve months ago was a miner in Wales or a mill-hand in Lancashire can become.

Now I must conclude, or I shall have nothing to say next month! In my last letter I told you that the Vicar had kindly consented (having squared the Churchwardens) to a Fund at St. Barnabas to help this Station. There is one chronic complaint which you can all help to control. It is lack of cigarettes. True the Army rations include forty cigarettes on every Sunday morning. This kindly dole alleviates the complaint for some thirty-six hours, and then it breaks out vehemently again. I hear that Mr. Fraser[51] has kindly consented to organise the relief fund. I hope he will be overwhelmed by offers of assistance. We also want monthly and weekly magazines and illustrated newspapers (not more than a week old, please). Support the Fag-Mag. Fund.

I hope that you are establishing firmly that second link between St Barnabas and the C.C.S [casualty clearing station]. We do indeed need your prayers. I often wonder in the early morning how many people are kneeling in the Chapel at St. Barnabas' to support the men out here by their prayers at the altar. Don't you fail them. Good-bye.

    I am,

        Yours sincerely,

            S. F. Leighton Green

Letter 2

                                 Somewhere in Flanders

           [written at CCS 22, Bruay,[52] Pas de Calais, France]

                   Palm Sunday [Sunday 16 April 1916]

Dear People,

    First of all, let me thank you for the first parcel of goods for this station from the "Mag-Fag" Fund. I have received four boxes of cigarettes, and a parcel of magazines, all very excellent, in first rate condition. If you could only see the faces of recipients as I go round the ward with your cigarettes and magazines, you would go off at once and pay another subscription to Mr. Fraser. In the name of the sick and wounded soldiers here, I thank you all very much indeed.

    Let me try and describe a day at this station, more especially from the point of view of a Chaplain. Reveille sounds at 5.30, and the R.A.M.C. unit parade at 6. Officers breakfast at 7, and at 9 the doctors pay their visits to the wards. At any time during the day or night, ambulances may arrive bringing in sick and wounded men either from Field Ambulances nearer the front, or from the various bodies of troops which are stationed at every village in the area occupied by the British Army. Whenever an ambulance enters the courtyard, a bell is rung; and every one concerned proceeds to the receiving-room, and the orderly officer of the day proceeds to examine the patient. In a short time the patient is relieved of his clothes, kit bag and rifle, and finds himself tolerably comfortable on a stretcher on tressels with good sound blankets to cover him. Dinner at 12, tea at 4 p.m. for patients with rations as prescribed by the doctor. If any of you know sick or wounded soldiers out here in hospital, you can be quite at rest on this point that sick or wounded get first-class diet, and plenty of what the army knows as "medical comforts." Indeed, many a soldier has told me that his food and general treatment in hospital is some compensation for being sick or wounded. The afternoon is usually the time for operations, although the surgeon is prepared to operate at any moment. We have a very brilliant young surgical specialist from Canada on the staff, and in cases of perplexity he can call in as consultants some of the very best surgeons England can produce. They are here with the army in the field for this very purpose.

The Chaplain is free to visit at all times when the doctors are not in the wards. He, of course, finds out all the critical cases, and much of his time is taken up with them, and especially by constant attendance on the dying. It is his duty to take down the last messages to the people at home, to write, perhaps, the last dictated letters, to receive instructions as to how the dying soldier wishes to dispose of the few personal possessions he has out here, and to see that those wishes are carried out. He ministers as a priest to the dying man, and when all is over he buries him in this strange land. A soldier's funeral here is always a very pathetic ceremony. Your thoughts go over the sea to the people at home, and you think of the sorrow that will never leave them while life lasts. Then, too, you are burying the very best, the strongest and fittest of our manhood. This is a sad and tragic side of war. I do not forget the glorious side – the touch of glory tingeing the dark cloud, and the glory of great sacrifice. "Greater love hath no man than this, that a man lay down his life for his friends." The daily experience of a Chaplain here gives intense meaning to the words we use at the offering of the Eucharist, "Let us pray for the sick and wounded, for the dying, for the anxious and the bereaved and those who have fallen in battle."

But there are sick and wounded who, please God, will soon recover, be sent home or go back to duty; some virtually convalescent from some slight illness or slight wound. They do not stay here long, as I have said, sometimes only a few hours, a day or two at the most. Here the Chaplain engages in friendly talk, hears of all their glorious deeds and thrilling experiences. He must needs be a good listener, there is little need for him to talk when once the ice is broken. At this point, your cigarettes and papers come in useful to cement the friendly relationship established. Here again the Chaplain can be useful in writing the letters dictated by men whose hands or arms are swathed in bandages and in other ways besides. A soldier boy said to me the other day, "Will you write a letter for me to my best girl?" I did – it was not very exciting after all, but I shall not tell you what he said. From all this you will see that many hours a day, and some at night, are taken up with manifold ministrations to the patients of the C.C.S. The Chaplain has other duties, but this is his first charge.

Lights out in hospital at 8 p.m. The R.A.M.C. unit retire at 9 p.m. to bed to sleep the sleep of the just, for they have been busy from early morning with all the routine work of a large hospital, carrying stretchers, cooking, washing, scrubbing, assisting in various wards with a thousand other things beside. Lights out, 9.30 p.m. No one but officers can be about after that except the night orderlies under the night sister. Then the Chaplain begins his official correspondence, official returns, letters to the homes of sick and wounded, letters of sympathy with the bereaved, answers to anxious enquiries, and when this is done, he turns in.

I will tell you some more next month. I think this is quite enough for May. Good-bye. Remember us all in your prayers.

I am,

Yours very sincerely,

S. F. Leighton Green

Letter 3

Somewhere in France
[written at CCS 22, Bruay, Pas de Calais, France]
2nd Sunday after Easter [Sunday 7 May 1916]

Dear People,

Since I last wrote another consignment of cigarettes and magazines has arrived from St. Barnabas', and that consignment has also vanished. We now want some more cigarettes, please. Very many thanks to you all for your kindness.

In my last letter I tried to give you some glimpse of the life at a C.C. Station from a Chaplain's point of view. I spoke of the primary duties of a Chaplain and the first claim upon his time. But there are secondary claims upon his time and energies – claims which he is glad to meet so far as possible.

(1.) *Field Censor.* – This is no essential part of a Chaplain's duty, but it is a duty he is usually asked to undertake by the Commanding Officer, and I was appointed Field Censor No. 1,504 soon after my arrival. The Censor's duty is to read, sign, and stamp with his official stamp all letters from patients and his R.A.M.C. unit. It is sometimes a heavy task. The daily letter bag from here totals from 100 to 250 letters. The Censor is pledged to secrecy as to the contents of the letters which come before him, but he is bound to erase all information forbidden by the regulations governing correspondence from the Front; in fact, everything that you at home desire to know most, but are not supposed to know. The Censor is therefore a very trying person.

You can imagine that it gets at times a very monotonous task – this multitude of letters to parents, brothers, sisters, cousins, uncles, aunts, and sweethearts. But it is good to be a Field Censor for two reasons. First, he is sometimes humiliated to the dust by reading the frank criticisms concerning himself and his sermons expressed by those who are not aware that the preacher on Sunday is Field Censor on Monday. Thereby he gets a fund of information. Then, secondly, he notes the never-failing courage and cheerfulness of the sick and wounded soldier who makes light of his injuries in order to relieve the anxiety of people at home. Indeed, I read daily the letters of patients here who give no address but that of their regiment, so that people at home do not know they are sick or wounded. It is done simply to spare their friends worry and anxiety. They recover and go back to duty, and no one in England is any the wiser. Sometimes it is impossible to do this, and then there is the keenest anxiety that their condition should be described as favourably as possible and put in the best possible light. A lad with frightful wounds has often asked me to write that he has got a "scratch or two." There is no grumbling, no complaining; just brave endurance and consideration for others. The Censor, so to speak, has his hand on the pulse of the soldier, and knows that things are all right with the spirit and temper of the Army. What a lesson it is to all grumblers and croakers!

(2.) *The Canteen.* – A second outlet for spare energy is the R.A.M.C. Canteen, of which I have become a sort of general manager. I run a general business, with a turn-over of hundreds of francs a week. I am acquainted with all the breweries in the neighbourhood, and am supposed to be (though I am not) an authority on the quality of the beverages they produce. I pay a periodical visit to a British Field Force Canteen some five miles away, and I here have large supplies of tinned salmon and herrings, fruit, chocolate, cakes, camp coffee, boot polish, boot-laces, biscuits, soap (Monkey Brand), all of which things are retailed in our canteen. I think I have purchased enough stuff to supply the whole British Army, but it all disappears in an incredibly short time. The edible part of the purchase vanishes like the provisions of a Sunday School treat. The canteen is practically the R.A.M.C. Club, and I try to get in for a few minutes each night in order to smoke a pipe with the handful of men off duty. The canteen is a capital thing, and does a world of good. Our R.A.M.C. men work hard, and in spare moments they like to get there. It keeps them together, and makes for the spirit of comradeship.

(3.) *Concert Manager*. – Once a week we try and scratch up a concert party for the benefit of the patients. Sometimes we are reduced to local talent supplied by the R.A.M.C. men, and I think they do very well. At times we are able to pick up "star" turns from units around. We have had really good luck in this way. After all, some of the best talent England can produce is now in khaki and out here. We find a captain of A.S.C. [Army Service Corps] who before the War was a noted pianist, a subaltern in the R.F. [Royal Flying] Corps who was an actor, and a sergeant who was an operatic singer. A week or two ago we got a captain from an Australian battalion, and he kept us going with recitations in first-rate style. Occasionally we have a string band – a battalion has enough talent in it to get one going, and they are glad to give a hand to the Station. The duties of a concert manager are, on the whole, not so very difficult out here. A few weeks ago we had a first-rate entertainment from one of Miss Lena Ashwell's concert parties.[53] They are all pro-fessionals, who have been given permission to visit the troops in the field. They are really doing their "bit," and every soldier is grateful to them for coming. On rare occasions we get rather badly let down for artistes, and would be glad of the assistance of the "Merry Knuts" from St. Barnabas'.

Miss Lena Ashwell,
artiste and impresario

48

In conclusion, I have received from Mr. Varden[54] a copy of a very kind resolution passed by the Easter Vestry. Really the Vestry has nothing to thank me for. While I was Curate-in-Charge I only did my duty, and tried to carry on as best I could. No man could do less while his Chief was away at the Front. But I do thank you very much for your sympathy and help in my work out here. I have always held that at home there are easier jobs than the parson's, and it is the same out here. Had I been at that meeting I should just have wanted to say how grateful I was to the Vicar who so generously allows me to remain as Assistant-Curate of St. Barnabas' and at the same time to be a Chaplain to the Forces in France.

     I am,

          Yours very sincerely,

              S. F. Leighton Green

Letter 4

Somewhere in France
[written at CCS 22, Bruay, Pas de Calais, France]
Whitsunday [Sunday 11 June 1916]

Dear People,

     Thank you again for the cigarettes and the magazines. They are still very welcome, and of great service, and we could hardly have too many of them. I hope you will still continue to support Mr. Fraser, who so kindly runs the Fund. Very many thanks to the "Merry Knuts" for proceeds of their Entertainment.[55]

     Some two months ago the Station to which I am attached made a move. The British Army, as every one who has read the dispatch of Sir Douglas Haig knows, took over a part of the line held by the Army of France, and we moved in order to meet the needs of British troops in the new area. The process of moving is, as no doubt most of you know from experience, a very uncomfortable business at any time, and under any circumstances, and most of us here will remember the last days of March and early days of April as being one of the most uncomfortable times we have ever spent. They were days of wind, blizzard and snow – not ideal days on which to move. After much packing up and many preparatory journeys on motor lorries, we at last took farewell, and arrived finally at our new sphere.

     The town in which we are now stationed is a very dirty and smoky one in the midst of a colliery district.[56] The bulk of the population get their living in the coal mines. The normal population of the place is some 25,000, but today that figure has been doubled by the refugees from beyond the German lines who fled before the dreaded invader of their homes. A feature of the country around is the great slagheaps, which stand out like the Pyramids in the Egyptian desert. The town has been shelled from time to time by the German guns, and the effect can be seen in ruined buildings and damaged houses. However, the mines are worked day and night and the output of coal

Bruay-en-Artois and its surrounding slag heaps

is enormous. There are no holidays here for the miners. Coal is of tremendous national importance, one of the most important of the munitions of war. For the sake of France, the mines are worked unceasingly. No one thinks of holidays, no one dreams of strikes. So much for the town and its people.

We took over the premises occupied by the French Army Medical Service who had here "l'hopital d'Evacuation" which serves the same purpose as a Casualty Clearing Station. We are situated quite near the Railway Station on the outskirts of the town and the premises consist of long wooden huts. We have nine wards capable of taking fifty beds apiece, together with an operating theatre and other huts to meet the numerous requirements of the hospital. The men of the R.A.M.C. are under canvas with the tops of the tents painted red and green to evade the vigilant eye of the German aircraft observers. The officers and chaplains of the Station are billeted in French houses in the adjacent street.

The French have a peculiar genius for laying out premises like these, and they are in every way suitable for the purpose. The long wards are a welcome change from the small rooms of the Convent. In addition the proximity of the Railway line is a great asset, as the Hospital train comes alongside, so that patients can be taken on their stretchers and placed in the train in less than three minutes. This is a very great convenience, and it spares the patients lengthy journeys to the Station, and much suffering and discomfort are avoided thereby.

When we arrived there was no place for a Chapel. In the first week or two I had to hold Services in strange places, once in the operating theatre and once in the cookhouse. At last, as we got settled down, I was able to secure a marquee for a Church, and now it is known throughout the Station as the Chapel of St. Barnabas, —. I was able to get out from England a portable altar with frontal and dossal, and with the ornaments I had with me it presents quite a dignified appearance. Four stretcher tressels serve very excellently for altar rails. I have purchased carpets, mats and hassocks as required, and with the benches the chapel soon became as decent a place to worship in as we could possibly make under the circumstances. On one of my wanderings I found a conservatory and an old Frenchman insisted on my taking without payment some ferns in pots; which together with lilies of the valley from a little wood two miles away have adorned our little Sanctuary this Eastertide. The sides of the Church are adorned by sacred pictures, including one of the Saint to whom all France, and especially the soldier of France is devoted today, Ste. Jeanne d'Arc. The Chapel is as decent as we can make it. Here soldiers come to their Communion, and it is a private place which some of them, thank God, use for their private prayers when they are well enough to be up and about. Unfortunately, it has two defects. First, it is just two yards from the railway line, so that when an engine is pleased to let off steam just outside, during the time of Divine Service, I have just to wait till it is pleased to finish. Not being a Bishop, I am not perturbed unduly by such untoward noises. Then, secondly, it is rather small – we can only accommodate sixty or seventy at the most, so that there is rather a crush at the Service on Sunday evening. A piano does duty for an organ whenever we can find any one who can play it. Otherwise we sing without music. I daresay at times we are rather sharp, certainly at times we are very flat, but what matters? At least we sing as though we meant it. The reality of our Communion within sound of the guns makes up for much imperfection in external setting, and the praise of God is not less real because it is not very tuneful. We make at any rate a very joyful noise. You see in some cases to my knowledge – and this gives reality to things – a soldier's Communion here has been his last. He has gone back to the trenches, and been killed a

51

few days later. For how many soldiers crowded at Evensong on Sunday in our little Chapel, that Evensong may be a last act of worship, God only knows. This is true of services here in this Station, and still more true of services with the various bodies of troops I visit on Sunday. This uncertainty, not expressed may be, but for all this, often in our inmost thoughts, makes these Services very, very real, whatever the external conditions and surroundings may be. There is nothing conventional about such acts of worship. The services I hold are nearly always voluntary ones, as official parade services only come my way occasionally. They are, I hope and believe, truly the acts of men to whom God is becoming more and more the Great Reality and to whom the things that matter are more and more the real things of life. Remember us all in your prayers and at the altar.

  I am, yours sincerely,

    S. F. Leighton Green

P.S. – St. Barnabas' will be often in my thoughts, and in my prayers when you keep the Festival of our Patron Saint,[57] and I should like to be with you all then. All good wishes for a happy Festival.

Letter 5

Somewhere in France
[written at CCS 22, Bruay, Pas de Calais, France]
4th Sunday after Trinity [Sunday 16 July 1916]

Dear People,

  Last month I told you something about the Station. There is one Ward known as the Special Surgical Ward. The newspapers in England had reported that there had been a small night attack on our first line trenches and the enemy had occupied them. Later it was reported that we had made a successful counter-attack and the lost trenches had been regained. The Ambulance Convoy came in late in the afternoon. Dressings and bandages have been applied, operations have been performed, and things have settled down a bit. We will go now to the above-mentioned Ward. It is 11 p.m. There is a shaded light which dimly illuminates the long shed with its fifty beds. We will see some of the patients.

  Bed 1. Sapper A. —. R.E. [Royal Engineers], lies very still and quiet, his head bound and swathed in bandages and cotton wool. He seems to be asleep. He is quite unconscious and he will never speak again. He came in here like this with shrapnel wounds in the head. Nothing can be done for him. I must try and find out where he comes from and write to his relatives. A small muslin bag hangs by the bedside containing an identity disc, pay-book, pouch, pipe, matches, pocket-book, a few cigarettes, a bit of string, one or two buttons, a penny copy of St. John's Gospel, and any other personal and private property of Sapper A. Perhaps his home address can be found. In the pocket book is a letter enclosing a picture postcard. The letter begins, "My dear husband," and the picture postcard is a photo of two little children and addressed to "Dear Daddy." The letters give the address somewhere in England. I note the address and later write a letter to tell them all about it. Sapper A has been wounded, and the wounds are very serious indeed, and that I will write again to-morrow. The letter to-morrow will tell them that he had "died of wounds." I say the Prayer of Commendation and pass on, not without thoughts of the sorrow that will overwhelm that little home in England.[58]

Bed 2. A soldier here lies moaning in great pain, shot through the knee and ankle. His face is also bound with cotton wool – he was sprinkled with liquid fire. I look at the card over the bed. He belongs to an Irish Regt., and has an Irish name. His disc bears the letters, "R.C." – he is a Roman Catholic. I notice in his bag a piece of ribbon on a brooch taken from his tunic. It is red and blue and it is the ribbon of the medal for Distinguished Conduct in the Field.

"How long have you been out here?" – "All the time, sir."

"Been wounded before?" – "Yes, this is the third time."

"Where did you get your D.C.M.?" – "Neuve Chapelle, last May twelvemonth."[59]

"Have you seen your Chaplain here?" – "No, I saw Father — up at the trench after I was wounded."

"Well, there is one of your Chaplains here, and I will send for him." – "Thank you, sir."

"Good-night." – "Good-night."

Bed 3 is all screened in. There is a soldier here quite conscious, dying from abdominal wounds. Wounds of this kind are more fatal than any other. He knows he is going, the surgeon has told him he can do nothing, and that he had better see the Padre. He is very young, twenty perhaps, he is married – he married just before he came out. Well, he has messages for his wife and his mother, too, and they are quickly recorded. He gives me a matchbox out of his bag – that must go to his wife. It contains a ring she gave him when he left her, "for luck." So all their temporal matters get settled up. Then we try and get things in order for the next Parade – I cannot tell you any more than that. A few more minutes and his strength begins to fail and the face to fade. In the trenches two days later it is known that "Poor Young Billy has gone West."[60]

Bed 4. Private G. H., 2nd Batt., — Regt.

"Well, how are you, Private G. H.?" – "I am champion. I have lost my right leg in this scrap though."

"How old are you?" – "Seventeen, sir."[61]

"When did you enlist?" – "September 14."

"What were you doing then?" – "Well, I was at school. My brothers joined so I did."

"Well done, sonny. Is your mother living?"

"Yes, sir."

"Shall I write and tell her about you?" – "Well, – (great hesitation), tell her that it is nothing much or she will worry."

"But she will have to know?" – "Well, tell her later on. Just say I am wounded and doing champion."

"All right, sonny. Now, I will say a prayer before I go."

The prayer is said. – "Good-night, my boy." – "Good-night, sir."

11 a.m. next morning. A voice from No. 4. "Sir, I say, can you tell me how much pension I get for that leg?"

There are several others to see, but I will tell you about them another time. Perhaps these little stories, all of them true, will help you to pray more earnestly and oftener, even help you to get up early on a weekday and go to Church to pray for the sick and wounded and those who minister to them.

Yours very sincerely,

S. F. Leighton Green

P.S. – I have to thank you for two things. (1) Mr. Varden tells me you were kind enough to give me the Whitsuntide Offerings as in past years. Under the circumstances, I think it was particularly kind of you. You won't mind, I am sure if I devote some of it to the "Mag-Fag" Fund. Thank you all very much. (2) Many thanks for another parcel of cigarettes and a packet of magazines, etc. I am very much obliged to you all. I am looking out for the next consignment.

Letter 6

In a Casualty Clearing Station
[written at CCS 22, Bruay, Pas de Calais, France]
Trinity IX [Sunday 20 August 1916]

Dear People,

You will remember the Special Surgical Ward and the first four beds. We will visit the next three.

Bed No. 5. Corporal —, 17th Batt. —.

This battalion is the Footballers' Battalion.[62] A great, big chap lies in this bed – a guard bulges up the blankets over his right leg.

"Well, Corporal, how are you now?" – "Bad. This leg is done in. No more football for me. I'm a 'pro.' and play for —."

I look at the papers and see his thigh is shattered – always dangerous, these wounds. However the danger is not immediate, and I shall have many half-hours at this bedside. He fights for dear life for ten days, and then goes out. He has played the game. I doubt not he has won. A fine fellow – may he rest in peace.

Bed No. 6. Private F. C. — Batt., London Regt., TF [Territorial Force].

The doctor has told me something about this man. He asked me to tell him that he had had to amputate his right arm at the shoulder in order to save his life. He didn't know it as yet. These men quite commonly don't know they have lost a limb till they are told. They feel the arm or leg or foot long after it is gone.

"Well, how are you to-night?" – "Oh, I am all right if I could get some sleep. We had a rough time up at — and I got hit by a rifle grenade in the arm. The doctor up there said I should lose it. Do you think they can save it here?"

"Ah, it was very bad. The doctor here did his best, but it was hopeless. I am sorry, old fellow, but you have lost it." – (A hopeless look. I try and say something to comfort him.) – "Whatever shall I do," he proceeds, "I am a clerk in the Civil Service, and I'm organist at St. — Church, —." His eyes fill with tears as he says all this.

"Well, we will talk about this to-morrow. You want sleep now, and they are just coming to give you a dose to relieve the pain and make you sleep. Can I do anything for you to-night? Letters or anything?" – "Yes – my mother. Break it to her gently, won't you? You will find the address in my bag."

"Yes, all right, anyone else?" – "Yes, Miss A — B —, she is my – my –."

"Yes, yes, I know. Where does she live? I will write to her. Don't lose heart, old fellow. Time will help you to readjust things in your life. Trust God through it all. You are a Communicant, I suppose, at St. — Church." – "Yes."

"Well, I will come on Thursday, and bring the Blessed Sacrament if you wish." – "I should very much. I went out here at Christmas, but I haven't had a chance since."

"Here comes that dose. I will say a prayer with you before I go." – "Good-night."

Next day we talk about the future – the possibilities of things, artificial arms, etc. In three days he has gone to the Base Hospital. Four days later I get a letter. "Dear Chaplain, I am writing this with my left hand. What do you think of it? I shall do it better next time. I have had a letter from Miss A. B. She says she is prouder of me than ever. Good-bye, Pte. F. C." It was very good writing indeed.

No. 7. A young soldier from Yorkshire – a Derby recruit.[63] He is mortally wounded and unconscious. The lad in Bed 8 was wounded at the same time, and as I go to Bed 7 he observes, "He is my pal, he is. I knew him in —. He wanted to join me out here and he came up ten days ago. He went up with me to the trenches last night – his first time in. I'm afraid he is bad. Hard luck, isn't it, first night?"

No. 7 died that night. There is a lot of hard luck out here. Only two hours. But in a short time he fulfilled a long time. Two hours is plenty out here to give all you have to give – the sacrifice of your life.

In conclusion, let me thank you for your continued support of the "Mag-Fag" Fund. I am very grateful to you.

I should like to say too how deeply I sympathise with those who mourn the loss of our gallant boys who have fallen in the "push." I hear that four members of the Ward of St. George have given their lives in the great cause – George Hardingham, Percy Syder, Cecil Pepper and Herbert Harvey.[64] We shall always be proud of them. May God bless them, and give them rest and peace after the battle. They have not died in vain, for when the day of final victory comes, and the cause of liberty, truth and justice on the earth is finally vindicated, it will be the day of triumph for all those who have not counted their lives dear unto themselves, but freely and gladly have given them up for us all. In the world beyond what joy in victory will be theirs.

I am, yours sincerely,

S. F. Leighton Green

I love you more then ever now Jack, because you're the man who's been there.

Comic postcard reflecting soldiers' anxieties about how loved ones would react to their wounds

Three Heigham lads killed in action in 1916: (Top) Rifleman Cecil Pepper, (left) Private Herbert Harvey and (right) Private Percy Syder

Letter 7

[Written at CCS 22, Bruay, Pas de Calais, France]
[Undated, probably written September 1916]

Dear People,

A Casualty Clearing Station Chaplain has a fixed anchorage, but, fortunately, he is not confined to home waters. He is told to roam at large in search of troops who have no Chaplain, and to give a helping hand to Chaplains of Divisions who may be understaffed or overworked. Consequently I have always had a squadron of the Royal Flying Corps to look after. I will tell you something of a squadron I have had since Easter, to which I have just said good-bye to my great regret.

The — Squadron of the Royal Flying Corps was made up of 25 officers and about 130 men.[65] The officers for the most part did the flying as pilots and observers. The rest of the unit kept the machines in good order and in good repair, and did the general work of the squadron – wireless, photography, etc. I found their aerodrome with a good landing-ground. The officers were billeted all about the place, the men slept in the hangars under the wings of their machines.

The work of the squadron was of all kinds. They acted as patrols along the lines, and as scouts beyond them, reporting all the information they could get to the proper quarter. They took photographs of the German trenches – a service of great value to the troops. The formation of the trenches, new works in process of construction, and many other useful items were thus revealed. They also directed the gunfire of our batteries by means of wireless communication. They signalled the whereabouts of troops, gun emplacements, batteries, camps, and what not. They pointed out what roads should be shelled, and at what points. They also took their full share of bombing raids on hostile aerodromes, billets, and places of military importance. A very busy squadron with a great name was No. —.

The life of the flying man is full of excitement and adventure. The officers who for the most part carry out this dangerous programme are generally most extraordinarily young, just boys most of them. The C.O., who was secretly called the "old man," by these youngsters, was of no great age – just 26 – a Major with the D.S.O., won in a great exploit at Neuve Chapelle.[66] Well, they just set about the job with a most extraordinary indifference to the risks they run, and they come back full of glee as though they had been to a picnic.

A squadron of the R.F.C. has its joys. There is the "joie de vivre" in their work. An airman goes on patrol, and returns two hours later, having run more risks than most of us manage to get into a whole lifetime. Maybe he has been attacked by Fokkers, driven them off, he has brought one down, or he has been out at night and lost his way, so he has to stay up in the air for fear of coming down beyond the German lines, and all the while he is wondering whether his petrol will last out till the daylight comes. But he is back, and all is well. Then this or that officer does an extra fine bit of work in a daring raid, in a scrap single-handed with half-a-dozen German craft, downs one, and gets safely home again. The General pays a visit to the squadron, and decorates the boy with the ribbon of the Military Cross and gives him ten days' leave. It is quite remarkable how many of these officers have ribbons, and never were decorations more richly deserved. There is a wonderful spirit of comradeship between the officers. It comes from sharing common dangers and facing common risks, and I suppose in no part of the Army is there such personal loyalty to one another.

But the squadron has its sorrows. On a hillside overlooking the aerodrome there rest the gallant members of the squadron who have not got back. One I knew very well, an observer. One evening he was out with his pilot when three large German battle-planes attacked them. The observer opened fire, when the gun became strangely silent. The pilot by skilful manoeuvres brought his machine out of action badly damaged, and safely landed beyond the British lines, only to find his observer still with his hands at the gun, but dead, shot through the head.[67] Two young officers rigged out for a flight at about 10 p.m. They told me they were just going out, and I left them with a cheery good-night. Later I heard the plane go up, and saw it pass overhead. It has not returned, and never will. It came down about midnight in No Man's Land – the land between the British and German lines; no one knows how or why. Both officers were killed, and the machine was afterwards destroyed by British gunfire, lest it should fall into German hands.[68]

So it is. Life out here is full of laughter and full of tears; comedy and tragedy getting strangely intermingled.

When the prayer is said in Church for the King's Forces, and especially for those "in posts of special peril," pray for the airmen that they may be protected, and that they may have an ever deeper consciousness that "underneath them are the Everlasting Arms."

Yours sincerely,
S. F. Leighton Green

P.S. – Many, many thanks for the "fags" – an extra large parcel this time. I should like another like it. Go and see Mr. Fraser again, will you?

Letter 8

[Written at CCS 22, Bruay, Pas de Calais, France]
Trinity XVII [Sunday 15 October 1916]

Dear People,

It is wonderful how much the thoughts of the soldier in France centre on this one absorbing topic – his leave.[69] He talks about it every day, he writes about it every week, and month after month he looks forward to it even when the prospect seems very remote and far away. It is not that he fights less vigorously or shirks his job because his thoughts turn again and again towards leave. But leave means home, it means a brief spell of comfort, a comfortable bed for instance which is more than hundreds and thousands of men have enjoyed for endless months.

Well, at last the longed-for day arrives, and with full kit and rifle you see the soldier mount a bus or set off on a long tramp to catch the leave train. Of all the arrangements in France the worst managed concern is the leave train. It crawls slowly along – how slowly only those who have been in it know. It stops at countless stations picking up a few here and a few there, and often it seems to stop for no reason at all, sheer "cussedness" it appears. At last the Base is reached. The boat has gone for the day, so now there is a weary

'Ladies first': troops waiting to board the leave boat for Blighty

60

march to a rest camp for the night. Next morning the leave boat is alongside the Quay, and off we start across the Channel. We don't shout and we don't sing, but we count the hours and minutes before we get home. We notice things and yet we do not notice them. There is the escort of destroyers to see us safely over. Here comes the Hospital Ship from England on her return journey, and there is a troopship with reinforcements going out for the first time. At last the white cliffs of England come in sight, then we cheer with a right good will. A little later we are there and at the Coast Station bound for London. This is a better train, it moves, and in less than two hours we are in Town. The train carries 1,500 or 2,000 men, and ten minutes after arrival the platforms are clear, and the men have vanished, in all directions. That night they are home. The dreams and hopes of months are being realised. It is joy – the joy of getting home.

A week or ten days later, the crowd slowly reassemble at the London terminus. It is a wonderful scene, the return of the leave train with the men going back to the trenches. Many have their friends and relations to see them off. Here is a soldier and the whole family have come, each member carrying some bit of his equipment. Here is another with his wife and the baby in her arms. There is a boy and the girl by his side is his sweetheart. Here they all are, officers and men rapidly collecting from all parts of the United Kingdom. Time moves quickly now, and now it is up. "Take your seats, take your seats," shout the railway officials. What a moment it is, when those last good-byes and farewells are said. There is real courage in the men and real pluck in their womenfolk. "Good-bye." Will it be good-bye for ever? For some, yes, perhaps for many. God only knows. But it is over, and we are out of the station, the last shout out of hearing, the last fluttering handkerchiefs out of sight. Men sink back into their seats, but dare not look into each other's eyes. They say strained things, then relapse into a corner and pretend to sleep or look at a paper without seeing it. In fact, they do anything to hide the thoughts and feelings of that moment. Truly a moving scene is the departure of the leave train from the London terminus.

At last the coast is reached. It is getting dusk when the ship's horn sounds and out at sea we see the destroyer escort come to station. Very quickly in the gathering dusk the white cliffs of England vanish from sight. Then lights appear on head lands in front, and France is coming into view. As we get closer the harbour lights are switched on, and the crowded steamer comes alongside. The leave train is waiting, and means an all night journey in the same slow weary way. At each station a party gets out and the company gets smaller and smaller, as the hours go by. About midnight, the oil lamps grow very dim and then go out leaving us to finish the journey in the darkness. At 3 a.m. we stop at the station of a country town, the train has finished its journey and goes no further. The last party, half asleep, all stiff and drowsy, stumble about in the darkness. For some superior officers cars are waiting, for others they will come, some go and wake up the people in the Hotel de la Gare just opposite, and others set off in the darkness as they have some miles to go. A few hours later, everybody is back at his job, in the trenches, with the batteries, at the aerodrome, in the ambulance, or wherever it may be.

The long looked for leave is over – a thing of the past. Shall I say we are a little down-hearted? Perhaps so, little wonder if we are. With all its discomfort, was it worth while? A thousand times, yes. Well, anyhow we have to live in its memories now, for no one in the wide world can say when the next leave will be. Such is leave for the soldier.

I am,
Yours sincerely,
S. F. L. Green

P.S. – Many thanks (1) for the Cigarettes to hand and the Mags, and (2) for all the kindness of your welcome at S. Barnabas' – a happy memory.

Letter 9

[Written at CCS 22, Bruay, Pas de Calais, France]
Trinity XX [Sunday 5 November 1916]

Dear People,

At this time of year, you at S. Barnabas' are thinking about Confirmation which takes place before Christmas and it is about Confirmation out here in the Field that I want to tell you this month.

Many hundreds of British soldiers are confirmed out here in spite of the very difficult conditions of active service. The Chaplains with Divisions, at Clearing Stations, and at Base Hospitals are always anxious that men who wish to do so should become candidates and be confirmed as soon as possible. Of necessity, the period of preparation must be short, and it is often carried on under most difficult conditions. Chaplains with Divisions have prepared candidates in their dug-outs in the trenches, and behind the lines it is not always easy to get the necessary time and quiet midst all the claims upon a man's scant leisure when on active service. I have prepared candidates for Confirmation in a hangar at an aerodrome aided by the clear light of a candle. I have climbed up rickety stairs into an old and broken-down hay-loft to find another candidate, and as there was no seat we have shared blankets on the floor. I have prepared night orderlies in hospital with all the patients slumbering around, and in many other curious circumstances the work gets done. You have to take the men one by one as and when you can get them. The war does not stop because you want to hold a class. Perhaps it is possible to get in three short Instructions; seldom is it possible to do more. But as I think of the dozen soldiers I have prepared for Confirmation, no heart could wish for keener or more attentive candidates. It requires a fair amount of pluck to give in your name, a considerable sacrifice of very scant off time for the Instruction, and much real grit to hold on afterwards midst all the distractions of war. But these hard conditions, together with the constant realisation that the border line between life and death is very, very narrow, make for reality and serious purpose. May God give them all grace to persevere under the difficult and trying conditions out here, and the greater difficulties and temptations which may come to them when they get back home. Here is one reason why there should be a National Mission,[70] to make England a better England in order that the men who have come out on the side of religion out here may not be "put off" by the conditions when, please God, they get back. That is the great responsibility resting on all at home.

Church service attended by King George V in a commandeered French village theatre

Then comes the day of the Confirmation. A fortnight ago I went with some candidates to a Confirmation at a country town some five miles behind the trenches. It was held in a large room in the theatre, which had suffered considerably from a recent bombardment. The windows were all boarded in, and one could observe all the usual traces of war on every side. A temporary Altar had been erected in the room, and in front of it was a chair for the Bishop. The gathering together of the candidates was a memorable sight. Every candidate was a soldier; every branch of the Army seemed to be represented. Here were a group of men from the R.F. Corps. Here were men from Batteries, Supply Columns, R.A.M.C., and other services; but most striking of all was the arrival of some fifty men direct from the trenches, covered in mud from head to foot, and carrying the shell shrapnel-proof helmets. I suppose there were about 150 candidates together. Each little group was accompanied by an Army Chaplain.

At the time appointed the Deputy Chaplain General to the Forces, Dr. Gwynne, Bishop of Khartoum,[71] entered the room attended by the Senior Chaplain of the Corps in the district. There was a small portable harmonium to lead the singing, and we began with the hymn, "My God, accept my heart this day," very vigorously sung. Shortly afterwards the Bishop gave his address – a thoroughly practical, simple, manly address which it was good to hear. He emphasised the sternness of the conflict out here in the field. The conflict involved in our Baptismal Vows was no less stern. That warfare was indeed spiritual, and needed spiritual weapons. He dwelt on the need of holding on to

Deputy Chaplain-General, Bishop Gwynne

God by prayer and the Blessed Sacrament. It was very simply illustrated by many of the Bishop's own experiences out here during the two years of the war, and as I said it was good to hear. We sang "Our Blest Redeemer" kneeling, before the laying on of hands, and then these grand fellows knelt to the grace of Confirmation.

The hymn, "Soldiers of Christ arise" and concluding prayers brought to a close a very remarkable service.[72] The Bishop shook hands with every soldier present, and in an hour or so they were back in the trenches, at the battery, the aerodrome, the hospital or wherever their job might be.

It was good to think that night of the men confirmed in the field on active service. If God spares them to come back, we hope and trust that will be a re-inforcing power in the ranks of the Communicants. If it is theirs to return no more, what joy it is to think that out here they sought and found the grace of Him Who in life and death is the Hope and Strength of all Christian souls.

Yours sincerely,

S. F. Leighton Green

P.S. – Many thanks for the cigarettes. We want a parcel for Christmas.

Letter 10

[Probably written at Laventie, Neuve Chapelle sector, France]
Advent II [Sunday 10 December 1916]

Dear People,

Since my last letter to you, I have been removed from the Casualty Clearing Station and I find myself a Brigade Chaplain.[73] Naturally I was very sorry to leave because I had made many friends, but – in the Army when you get an order to move it is no use arguing about it – the only thing to do is to move. Last Sunday, after a last celebration in the little Chapel I have described to you, I was carried away in a motor on a journey of 20 miles to the Head Quarters of my Brigade.

I am now in a little town two miles behind the line. It is one of those many towns here that make you feel how terrible is the ruin of war. I suppose that just over two years ago it was a thoroughly prosperous and happy place. Today it is very largely in ruins.[74] The troops are billeted in what remains of the houses and shops. Many houses are just a heap of bricks, many have just one wall standing. The Church, which must have been a very fine one in the days of peace, is now absolutely in ruins. Parts of the walls remain and you can see shattered remnants of the stained-glass windows. The few French people who remain in the place have to worship in a temporary building and I often see the old Curé, who still remains at his post, visiting the few folk who are left in his parish.

I have two Battalions of Territorials to look after.[75] They are really splendid young fellows and already I feel a kind of pride at being Chaplain to such a fine crowd. I have no doubt it will take a long time to get to know them all but I hope that in time we shall be the best of friends. Today I had a Church Parade of one of my Battalions and I had a congregation of 350 men. I wish we had such congregations in our Church in England. My other

Battalion is holding the line – very busy at present as I know by the rattle of machine guns and the whistle of shells as I am writing this letter.

In spite of the fact that we are so near the line, it has been possible to put up a Temporary Church in the town.

It is the Church of "S. George on the Western Front," for the use of the Brigade. It was quite filled by the men this morning. The benches are rather rough, the piano is very much out of tune and it was certainly rather cold and draughty. The Altar is the best part of the Church. It has a Crucifix and two Candles and it stands out clearly with its red background and frontal. Anyhow the Chaplain here today is very grateful to his predecessors in the place for such a useful building. It has been used by the troops of many Brigades which have come to hold this part of the line, and it may well be that it will be used by many who come after us.

I am afraid this letter will be published too late to wish you happy Christmas but not too late to wish all at S. Barnabas' a happy New Year. Let us pray that 1917 may see our arms victorious and the restoration of a rightful peace. My thoughts and prayers be with you at the Altar on Christmas morning, and I am sure you will remember us in this strange land.

I hope, too, that the Vicar will agree to the carrying on of our "Mag-Fag" Fund in the interest of my Battalions. In the trenches both run short from time to time and I shall always be glad to fill my pack with cigarettes and magazines as I go on my wandering in the trenches. If he agrees, I hope you see Mr. Fraser as soon as possible. Many sincere thanks for the help you gave me at the C.C.S.

    With best wishes.
        I am,
            Yours sincerely,
                S. F. Leighton Green

Letter 11
        [Probably written at Riez Bailleul, Neuve Chapelle sector, France]
           Feast of the Circumcision [Monday 1 January 1917]

Dear People,

I expect you would like to hear how some of us spent our Christmas at the front. I can only tell you what I experienced myself with the Battalion, but I imagine it was the experience too of a good many others.

On the day before Christmas Eve, we left the trenches to go into billets. The trenches had become very uncomfortable owing to the prevalent wet weather, and we were glad enough to leave them. We had to march six or seven miles to a very scattered village somewhere about two miles behind the line.[76] There was a head wind, which at times almost brought us to a standstill. The roads were flooded in some places, and the mud was more than ankle deep in others, so you can imagine it was a very wet, muddy, dirty and tired battalion when we arrived at the end of our journey as night fell. The village, as I said, was very scattered, and the officer responsible for getting us all into billets had all his work cut out, but at last we all got under some sort of roof, and as the battalion cooks had gone on before, all the men were able to have a hot meal before settling down for the night. For the most part, we were in barns and farm outhouses, some of them in fair condition, others anything but comfortable.

I found a part of a barn unoccupied as a billet, and here I managed Service for Christmas Eve. The Pioneer Sergeant very quickly put up an altar, and here I was able to celebrate on Christmas Eve. We had also a short evening service. The Commanding Officer wanted a parade on Christmas Eve.[77] The nearest place for it was a Church Army Hut three miles away and here we went for the Parade Service – 800 strong with the battalion fifes to accompany the hymns.

On Christmas morning there were two celebrations of Holy Communion in the barn at 6.30 and 7.30. It was the most central place for the purpose, and I had a little congregation of the faithful at each celebration. We had to illuminate the place with many candles, and there on the rough floor the men knelt during the service. We sang the usual Christmas hymns with much enthusiasm, and we prayed for all those worshipping in our churches at home. The surroundings were very poor and mean, but we remembered the lowliness attending the Nativity at Bethlehem, and we felt we were one with the Shepherds who found Our Lord in a stable and cradled in a manger.

At 8.30 I was called away to help a brother Chaplain, I found him and his men also in a barn. The altar was made up of biscuit boxes in the centre and about 150 men knelt in a circle round it, and I assisted in administering the Blessed Sacrament to this splendid congregation. Then it was time to go and find my other Battalion, who were stationed some eight miles back, and I was glad to have secured an ambulance to take me there. There I found that the Adjutant had made arrangements in the Canteen Hut for a Celebration and over 100 men had assembled for the service. We sang the Christmas hymns and the Creed, etc., to Merbecke,[78] although we had no instrument of any kind. Everybody seemed to know it, and everyone sang splendidly. I shall have very happy memories of this Christmas Eucharist at the front.

I got back to the village at about 12, of course next thing was the Christmas dinner. I think every man had a very good one – Beef, Pork, Christmas Pudding, Oranges, Nuts and French Beer. Some detachments seemed to have secured a chicken and in one case I saw a duck. That every man had a good time was due to the officers, whose care for and interest in the men under their command is beyond all praise, and the men thoroughly appreciated the fact. In the afternoon there was a football match, and then in the evening it seemed that each billet had arranged a sing-song.

Needless to say at such a time our thoughts went over the sea to England, and we all hoped that the next Feast of the Nativity would find us back again. May that hope be fulfilled. Let us all pray for peace – rightful and abiding – a *victorious* peace before Christmas comes again.

I am,

Yours sincerely,

S. F. Leighton Green

Letter 12

[Probably written at Croix Barbée, Neuve Chapelle sector, France]

Sexagesima [Sunday 11 February 1917]

Dear People,

My letter this month must be a short one; it is not at all easy to write any letters at all in the trenches, and the letter I write for the Magazine is usually a very long one.

We have been having a very severe spell of cold weather. The French people say that they have not had such a frost for over 20 years. For weeks now the whole country has been covered with snow, and all the streams and ditches are covered with ice many inches thick.

The cold weather is very trying for the troops. When we are in the trenches it is not possible to keep warm because it is impossible to move about very much, and it is not always possible to have much of a fire because the smoke might attract the unpleasant attentions of the enemy over the way. So we have been very cold in the line. When we are out of it the billets in which we live are chiefly barns and farm outhouses made of wood and plaster. Consequently here again fires are often out of the question. The roof is not always very sound, and manifold cracks and holes in the walls admit the cold air at night. We all long for a good English fireplace with plenty of coal to burn in the same.

At present I am living in a farm. Perhaps some of you have seen the picture by a soldier out here in which he depicts a ruined shed, just a few sticks standing, a dead horse, and a few dead chickens. He is sitting on a biscuit tin writing home. The title of the picture is, "I am staying at a farm-house."[79] [See p.20] Well, the farm-house I am staying at is not quite so bad as that. Three sides of it have been blown away, but a stable on the other side still remains. That stable has been patched up with canvas and sandbags, and made into quite a respectable home for two officers and myself. There we have our meals, and here at odd moments we sleep. In this room I am scribbling this letter, by the light of a candle stuck into the neck of a bottle. It is wonderful how ingenious people become at the front, and how essential things are made out of the most unlikely material.

I am very much obliged to you for the cigarettes. Once we get into the trenches it is difficult, except under exceptional circumstances for the men to get out to buy what they want. Consequently cigarettes run short, and then it is that your parcel comes at a critical moment. A cigarette makes all the difference when you are cold, and have to stand about, and somehow or other we view a bombardment in a different light if we have a cigarette between our lips. Hence the gratitude your parcel earns.

With many thanks,
I am,
Yours sincerely,
S. F. Leighton Green

Letter 13

[Probably written at Beaudricourt, Arras sector, France]
[Undated, probably written mid-March 1917]

Dear People,

I remember reading some time ago a poem written by an officer who had been on the Gallipoli Peninsula, and the subject of his poem was his "dug-out" in the trenches. When the time came to leave it, he was so moved that he broke out into verse.[80] Well, I don't know whether the dug-outs there were much better than those out here, but I do know that when the time comes for us to leave them there are very few who will say good-bye to them in regretful verse.

My first dug-out, shared with two other men, was very low-roofed, and one had to crawl into it as best one could. Inside it was just possible to sit upon the floor. The beds were boards raised about a couple of inches from the ground. However, it was fairly dry, thanks to a concrete floor, and it was free from water. On the roof were banked many layers of sandbags and earth. It would have required a fairly heavy shell to have knocked it in. There for six days we had our meals and slept. It was home for the time being, so we adorned its walls with pictures cut out of magazines. It became quite a home of culture and refinement.

Another dug-out I remember was semi-circular in shape, made of iron and then covered with earth. Here it was possible to sit upon boxes – the only chairs, and down the centre ran a roughly made table. In many dug-outs if you have a fire you must suffer many things from the smoke because there is no chimney, but this one had a brick chimney which conducted the smoke outside. Along the sides were shelves about three feet wide, on which at night we stretched ourselves, even if we did not sleep. This was luxury.

The third dug-out I will roughly describe was rather underground, and consequently it tended to become full of water. Every hour or two we had to get to the pump, or else we should have been flooded out. At night we had to place a sentry at the entrance to watch the rising water, or we might have been drowned. There are many dug-outs like this. They are not exactly pleasant places in which to live for a week.

There are inhabitants of the trenches other than the British soldier. We are outnumbered, I think, by rats. They infest the trenches in huge numbers, so that as you walk along the trench at night you tread upon them, or you can knock them down with your stick. They find their way to dug-outs at night on the look-out for any food. They run up and down the dug-out over your bed and everywhere. If disappointed in their search for food, they make up for their failure by just coming and biting your nose or hanging on to your ears, I remember waking one night with a rat hanging on to my nose. I have never liked rats since.

The other inhabitants, much more rare, are cats. They belonged to the ruined farm-houses in the vicinity – now mere ruins, or just a heap of bricks and mortar. They have found a home in the trench and they live on rats and mice and scraps of food from the rations of the men. The trench cats are rather wild and warlike – they bite and scratch with great vigour. I suppose this is the result of the environment. Strange to say, they are quite unmoved by the noise of battle. The guns may thunder and roar, shells may burst all round them, but inside the dug-out the trench cat is undisturbed, and sleeps peacefully through it all. Well, these cats are handed on from battalion to battalion. My dug-out was a kind of Headquarters of the Cats' Company, for stuck up on the side of the dug-out I found this notice on the back of a Christmas card: –

TRENCH STORES.
Herewith 6 cats and 3 kittens, handed over in good condition. Please
take care of same, and hand over to successors.

So I became officer commanding cats. I paraded them at meal times, and
rationed them. At the end of six days, when we left the line, I, too, put up a
notice to those who followed us:

TRENCH STORES.
Herewith 6 cats and 3 kittens, in first-rate condition. Please ration and billet
the same, and hand over to successors. Chaplain, C. of E.

It was a great joy to be with you for a few days at St. Barnabas'. Thank
you for all your kindness and for your support of the Mag-Fag Fund.

All good wishes for a happy Easter.

I am,

Yours sincerely,

S. F. Leighton Green

Letter 14

[Probably written at Arras, France]

[Undated, probably written mid-April 1917]

Dear People,

I want to tell you something about Holy Week and Easter, as I
experienced them at the front. For some days before Palm Sunday [1 April]
we had been on the move from place to place, and I was afraid that the
prospects for Holy Week and Easter were not particularly good. On Palm
Sunday we arrived in a large village chiefly in ruins where people lived
mostly in the cellars.[81] However, there was one building which was more or
less intact, and that was the French Protestant Church. In some wonderful
way it had escaped the destruction meted out to the rest of the village. The
Parish Church was a heap of bricks, and the Churchyard was just a heap of
shattered tombstones. On my arrival I took over the French Protestant
Church for the use of the troops. In appearance it had all the peculiar
features of an English Nonconformist Chapel. At one end was a large pulpit,
just below it a reading desk, and in front of that a small table. I was able to
erect an Altar on that table. Fortunately, too, there was a small harmonium,
with one pedal broken, but capable of making sounds. There was a small

71

gallery at the entrance end, and the place seated about 180 people. We were most fortunate to have such a place for Holy Week and Easter.

We arrived late in the afternoon on Palm Sunday, and the only service I had on that day was an evening one at 6.30 p.m., but as the troops had had no food for some hours, and had only just arrived in billets I was not surprised that the congregation was very small. In addition they hardly had time to know there was a service. During Holy Week it was possible to hold several Celebrations each day, and as you know now Holy Week was a week full of preparations for battle. The men were very hard at work, and some of them had no opportunity for attending a service at all. However, the whole Brigade was in the neighbourhood, and at all the services we had good congregations. Each evening we held a service at 6.30 p.m., and the Chapel was usually crowded. Work went on as usual on Good Friday, but in spite of everything the Chapel was crowded three times in the course of the day, and so we commemorated the Lord's Passion. On Easter Even some of the troops of the Brigade moved away to their battle stations, and their places in the village were taken by others. On Easter Sunday morning I had five Celebrations, and about 180 Communicants. They were very uplifting services. At each Celebration we sang the Easter Hymns, and so we kept the Festival of our Lord's Resurrection.

Before the close of the last Celebration the village was heavily shelled, some of the men who had been at the previous Celebrations were killed, and many were wounded.

Two hours later the Chapel was in ruins as the result of the bombardment.[82] The dawn of Easter Monday saw the opening of the great battle of Arras. Many of the men who worshipped in that Chapel during Holy Week were laid to rest after the day's fighting. To those of us who survive those services will be a very sacred memory. I for one shall remember till my dying day those many groups of men kneeling on the stone floor of the Chapel to receive the Body and Blood of Christ, and then going forth to the battle in the strength of their Lord.

We are still in the fight. I hope you will remember us all constantly in your prayers.

Yours sincerely,
S. F. L. Green

Letter 15

[Probably written at Berneville, Arras sector, France]
[Undated, probably written mid-May 1917]

Dear People,

In my last letter I told you my experiences in Holy Week and Easter Day. As you know, Easter Monday saw the opening of the great offensive which is becoming known as the Battle of Arras. The Division I'm serving with took part in the opening stages of that battle, and was more or less continuously in action for twelve days.[83]

On Easter Monday morning [9 April] early I was standing at a point where one could view the country over which the advance was to be made. For days before there had been a continuous artillery preparation of most tremendous force. Guns in front of us and guns behind us, of all calibres, had been bombarding the German lines both by day and night. I remember the preliminary bombardment before the great attack last July,[84] but that seemed small when compared to this. It was difficult to think that anything could live in that zone of fire unless deep down under the earth, and as a matter of fact that is where the Germans had lived for days before the attack, with little or no food, because of the impossibility of bringing it up. At a given time the infantry attack was made on Easter Monday morning. I could hear the whistles of the Company Commanders, and then for miles on either side I saw wave after wave of our men go over the top in their advance on the German lines.[85] Presently the machine guns of the enemy began to open fire, and one could see gaps here and there in the wave, but still they pressed on till lost to sight either in the ruins of the villages in front or in valleys which hid them from view.

A few hours later I was at the Advanced Dressing Station, where the wounded began to arrive, and for the next sixteen hours there was a practically continuous stream. Again, I noticed what was very familiar to me in my Casualty Clearing Station days – the tremendous pluck and spirit of the wounded soldier. I was in the hut where stretcher cases were dealt with. Many, of course, were actually dying, for many others the hours of life were numbered, but in the main the wounds were such as not to endanger life even if they meant that fighting days were over. It was a sad business, but relieved again and again by the light spirit of the sufferers.

The next day I spent upon the battlefield – a perfect wilderness of ruins, mud and shell holes – a scene passing all description in its wretchedness and squalor. The weather made it worse – snow, sleet and rain only added to the misery of it all. We had grim work in hand – the searching for and collecting of the dead. Each Chaplain had a party of men to assist him in the work of

73

identity, of gathering together the personal effects, and then the burial of the body. We buried men on the battlefield, officers and men side by side in a long trench. The ground in which they rest is hallowed ground, its soil "shall be for ever England."[86] May God give rest and peace to their souls, and remember for good their great sacrifice. That night I rejoined my Battalion, busily engaged in consolidating the line. I could go on to tell you of the great counter-attack and its repulse, but my letter would be inordinately long. Suffice it to say that we lived through the never-to-be-forgotten days, living in mud and shell holes, feeding on dry biscuits and bully beef, sleeping when we could get the chance, and that was not too often. War is a squalid business in its exterior – mud, blood and tears and desolation. It is redeemed by the heroic spirit and the wonderful qualities manifested by the soldier.

I was grieved to read in last month's Magazine of dear John Moore's death in Mesopotamia.[87] It is another name on the Roll of Honour of the Ward of St. George. He was one of the very best who has died on the field of honour. We shall cherish all the other gallant boys in proud and loving memory.

Yours sincerely,
S. F. Leighton Green

P.S. – During the battle a Company Commander sent me a message: "Not a single man in my Company has had a cigarette for two days. Can you help me?" Fortunately I had one of your parcels in the rear. I sent for it and took it up, and earned undying gratitude. Well carry on, and buck up the Mag-Fag Fund and earn some more gratitude.

Tommies stopping for a fag after a fight, a relief of tension

Letter 16

Dear People,

I told you in my last letter something about the days we spent at Easter in the midst of all the horror and desolation of a battlefield. Those days were days of ceaseless strain and they call for all the endurance of mind and body we can muster. But there is always a limit to men's powers of endurance and sooner or later the division is withdrawn from the fighting line for a brief rest. I remember after twelve days of attacking, pushing and counter-attack with what a sense of relief we heard that we were going out and a fresh division was to take our place. We left the line – a weary, dirty, mud-caked crowd – many of us had not washed or shaved for many days. We went back just behind the lines from which we had started out before the great attack began. There we spent the night. The next day we were taken by lorry and by omnibus to a little village not far behind the line.[88] A year ago before the great battle of the Somme it had been a rest billet for the troops and along the road we came across the old pit where the heavy artillery used to be, but now the tide of battle had receded and left the place in peace. I remember with what a strange joy we saw the countless daffodils growing in the grass of the fields and along the hedges. It was still cold, but here was sunshine, and to see green grass again after the sticky brown mud of the battlefield was a welcome change – a thing good to see. The next day was a Sunday, and it was possible to hold Church parades in the open and I think they were the most real parade services I have known as yet. All of us there had so much to be thankful for, so much to pray about. We made a simple memorial of our comrades who had fallen in the fight and whose bodies we had left behind on the battlefield, commending their souls to God as into the hand of a faithful Creator and most merciful Saviour. Parade Services for many reasons are seldom very interesting but those on this day seemed to be the real thing, and it was good for us to be here. Our Celebrations too had the same spirit. Though held in a hut or in a barn, they were Eucharists indeed, and there was a new and vivid meaning in the words, "Come unto Me, and I will refresh you."

The following days were spent in cleaning up, going to the baths, and what a business cleaning up is after three or four weeks since last we were able to do it! They were spent in resting and how you can sleep after a fortnight of restless days and wakeful nights! The days after the battle I think are amongst the happiest the soldier knows. The Canteen is there and the

Recreation Room, and you can write a letter in comfort and somehow the fact of hardship, danger and suffering faced together does bind us somewhat in a closer fellowship. Men seem to me more lovable. I don't quite know why, but they are, I'm sure of it.

We had been promised ten days' rest, What hope! On the fourth as we were having dinner the order came, "You must be ready to march in an hour's time," and we found ourselves not going further back, but towards the front again.[89] Stage by stage we made the journey till by the time the 10 days were up we found ourselves on the way to the reserve lines again. We were in for it again. Once again we found ourselves in front of our guns, and as the shades of night fell, and we lay on the ground for the night the German shells begin to burst on the roadside. A splinter wounds one of our men – the first casualty is reported. Our rest time seems like a dream – we are back again at the war.

Since I last wrote to you, I have met one you all know. On Ascension Day [17 May], when we had just been relieved again, I was in a soldiers' club, and quite unexpectedly found myself face to face with Mr Schomberg.[90] He had to attend a meeting but we arranged to meet in the evening and we talked like women over a wash tub. He looked very fit and well and was just the same as ever, and he wished to be remembered to all his old friends at St. Barnabas'. It was a real pleasure to meet him again.

Two days later I was on the march with my Battalion. We entered a village as another Battalion left it, but I heard some welcome shouts: "Hullo, Mr. Green, hullo. How are you?" It was one of the Norfolk Battalion.[91] I recognised a boy from Armes Street, and a man from Heigham Street gripped me by the hand. Another, I didn't know who he was, started, "Are you from St. Barnabas? I know Mr. Lanchester," and then it was all over – our ways had parted. Quite an uplifting two minutes – I hope we may renew our acquaintance one day for a longer time.[92]

Many thanks for the parcel of cigarettes. I hope you will send another very soon. Look at these two notes: – [93]

> Dear Padre,
> Can you help us? We have been in this first line five days, there is not a fag amongst my men. The Boche is shelling like blazes.
>
> Yours, etc. A – B – Capt., O.C.C.Co. [officer commanding 'C' Company]

Letter 17

[Probably written in Denier, Hébuterne sector, France]
[Undated, probably written in mid-July 1917]

Dear People,

I want to tell you in this letter about our services at the front. Of course when we are in the trenches or active operations are taking place, and even when there is a lull in the proceedings, it is impossible to hold services of any kind. We are wholly and entirely occupied in the business in hand, and when, as at times happens, there would seem to be a possibility because everything seems quiet, Commanding Officers very rightly and wisely in my judgment, forbid a concourse of men to assemble. We are in the presence of the enemy, and one single shell might make casualties of the whole congregation.

But we will suppose that we are out of the line in what are known as "rest" billets, in, let us say, a peaceful French village some six or eight miles behind the line. What can be done? Well, first of all in the army there is the Church Parade of the Battalion. It is a compulsory service for all members of

Church Parade in the open before battle

the Church of England, and as much a Parade of the Battalion as any other, with the exception of the Roman Catholics and Nonconformists who do not wish to be present. All Jews too can claim exemption, but in these Battalions with which I deal I don't think 100 men are away from Church Parade. On Saturday night the Battalion orders make this announcement: –

"The Battalion will parade for Divine Service at 9.30 a.m. to-morrow on the Parade Ground."

After breakfast there is much cleaning up. "Spit and polish," the process is called in the army, and at 9 a.m. you find the Companies marching off in the direction of the ground. An Army Service is always punctual to the minute, and woe betide the Company arriving late, and even Chaplains are reported to have got into serious trouble for arriving late on the Parade ground. The Battalion is drawn up three sides of a square by the Sergt.-Major, and the band (if there is one) form the fourth side, and in front of the band, behind the drums covered with the Union Jack, the Chaplain takes his place. At the appointed time the Commanding Officer comes on to the ground, the whole Battalion is called to attention.[94] The Chaplain salutes the Commanding Officer, who returns his salute, and from that moment the Chaplain takes charge of the Parade and Divine Service begins.

The service in the Army Book appears to be a shortened form of Morning Prayer. We begin with a Hymn, and proceed as in the Prayer Book to the end of the *Venite,* which is sung. Then a lesson is read, usually by the Commanding Officer, and we sing the *Benedictus* and we say the Creed, Collects, some War Intercessions, the Prayer for St. Chrysostom and the Grace. There is another hymn, then the address. If it is at all possible and the ground is dry, the Chaplain requests men to sit on the ground. If it is wet they stand for the Address. An Army Commander who once addressed the Chaplains, said that in his opinion the first requisite in a good sermon was brevity, and I think we generally agree with him – the sermon is short. It is not Sunday night at St. Barnabas. At the end of the address we sing a hymn, and the National Anthem, and then the Chaplain gives the Blessing. He then salutes the Commanding Officer, who takes over the Parade again. In a few seconds the band is at the head, the Battalion marching in fours off the ground. Divine Service, as the Army understands it, is finished for the week.

Now the Chaplain on Sunday morning may have to take two or three such Parade Services as I have described. In addition (thank God) he can arrange whatever voluntary services he likes. The voluntary services are Celebrations of the Holy Communion, and an Evening Service. The Celebrations usually arranged are at 7.30 and somewhere about 11.30 to 12 noon, as circumstances dictate. The trouble often is to find a suitable place. At this moment we have a barn – we have erected an Altar and made rough benches and here we celebrate the Holy Communion. The Altar is made of ordinary wood, and is covered with red cloth, and we have a reredos – a wooden framework also covered with red material. We have lights and a Crucifix, and a small credence table – a biscuit-box covered over. It is all very rough and ready, but it is the best we can do and we make the Altar as dignified as is possible under the circumstances.

At the Celebration we usually sing hymns, and on festivals we try to arrange to sing *Merbecke*. Sometimes we have music, usually we can't, but we do the best we can. Anyhow, some of our Eucharists out here on Sunday, with, perhaps, a congregation of 70 or 80 men, have been some of the happiest I have ever known. However much people may argue about it, the Eucharist is the highest act of worship. If any one doubts it, they should go from a Church Parade to the Holy Eucharist!!

There is also the Evening Service. Evensong is very popular out here, and we usually get over-crowded, and I fear some are turned away. We usually have the Service complete just as you have it at home, and the address can last for twenty minutes. If we remain for several days in a place we usually have a daily Celebration and a daily Evensong. It is only with difficulty men can come, but even when no men come it is good for the Chaplains, and I have met men who are glad in the thought that they at their various jobs are remembered at the Altar and in the prayers of the Church.

Yours sincerely,

S. F. Leighton Green

Letter 18

[Probably written in rest billets in the Ypres sector, Flanders]
[Undated, probably written early August 1917]

Dear People,

It is impossible to live for any length of time amongst people without receiving definite impressions about them, and so it has been with us out here, who have been for months amongst the people of France.

First of all, we have been impressed by the wonderful courage of the French people as they have faced the horrors of this war. The invader is still in their country, and controls some of their richest provinces. The losses of France in men and material have been stupendous, but today she is as resolute as ever to rid herself once for all of the menace which has overshadowed her life for forty years. Today she is confident of final victory.

The French people are patriots first and foremost. "La Patrie" to them is everything. "Mort pour la Patrie" they write over the graves of their fallen warriors. Patriotism means sacrifice to them, and no sacrifice is too great if only France can be served and saved. There is a story of a French peasant who called on the Mayor of his country town, and anxiously asked if he was sure that France would win. "Yes," replied the Mayor. "Are you quite sure?" asked the peasant. "Yes," said the Mayor, "absolutely sure." "It is well, I am content," replied the peasant. He had just received news that a son had fallen in the war. He had previously lost six. Seven sons for France! but worth while if France is victorious.

The French peasants are wonderfully hard-working people, and for the most part they are cultivators of the land. Of course, everyone who can serve in the Army has gone, and the work on the land has been carried on by the old men, women and children. They toil early and late; the results are amazing. I remember large fields, which, early in the year, were full of trenches, wire, and gun emplacements. Then came the advance, and the fields were liberated. Today there are crops of every kind growing in those fields. They carry on their work well within the danger zone. The shells scream over their heads at times, but quite unmoved they proceed with their daily task.

Then, again, the French peasants are very thrifty people. They seem to live on bread, vegetables, soup, and coffee for the most part. The result is that the peasants save a heap of money. They are very suspicious of banks and paper money. They like to keep the gold in their own possession, and it is often the case that when the country was invaded they buried their gold, and as the Germans retreat they are coming back to dig up their hidden treasure. The war at this moment is being carried on in France on the savings of the peasants, who were persuaded by the local authorities to invest their savings in the last War Loan. It was only then discovered how great was the wealth of the French cultivators of the soil. They went to the Town Hall on their carts carrying bags of gold, and there is no doubt that their response to the call for money was of tremendous value to France at a critical moment.

On the whole the French people have welcomed the presence of British troops, and done everything for their comfort. Their barns and outhouses are made into billets for men, and their houses billets for officers. For three years they have not been able to call their homes their own. In spite of all the British soldier is popular with the French people. "Vive les Tommies" is quite a common expression. There are many instances on record where the French women have mothered our English boys, and look after their best welfare. One hopes at least one of the great gains of the war will be permanent friendship between England and France. They have fought, suffered, and died side by side in the common cause, and one may hope that they will always hail each other as friends and Allies.

Yours sincerely,

S. F. L. Green

P.S. – I was very sorry to hear of another of the Ward of St. George being killed in action – Percy Mower.[95] He was one of the original members of the Ward, and his name is now added to the Roll of those who have made the great sacrifice. May God give rest to his soul, and comfort to those who loved him.

Letter 19

[Probably written in the trenches near Lagnicourt,
opposite the Hindenburg line, France]
[Undated, probably written in September 1917]

Dear People,

During the last few months I have spent many days and weeks in the ruined villages of France. War in these days is a destructive thing, and I doubt whether any words can adequately describe the desolation and ruin of the villages in the internal war zone. There is a village on the Somme which had a population of several hundred people absolutely obliterated by shell fire. The bricks of the houses were reduced to powder, and as you pass along the road through the main street there is absolutely nothing to show that a village ever existed.

In the course of the German retreat and the British advance this year there has been, so far as I know, nothing quite like that, but one passes village after village in utter ruin. There is not a house with a roof over it or without shell holes in its walls. Sometimes there is nothing but a heap of bricks, stones, and rubbish. In the midst of the heap you may find pieces of furniture, bedsteads, and odds and ends of household utensils. Everything is smashed and broken. A feature of French villages in this part of the country is that they are well wooded, and quite hidden in the summer months by the trees surrounding them. Many of these trees had been cut down by the Germans for military purposes, but those remaining have been cut down to mere stumps by shells, and all you can see is a small piece of the trunk split and splintered. Then the gardens are a scene of desolation. I went one Sunday morning recently behind a ruined house, and found the most beautiful rose trees blooming, but, for the most part the gardens are nothing but a mass of shell holes. The hedges, the flower beds, the paths, all show the effects of gunfire. They have been transformed for the most part into a wilderness. A war-swept village is a pathetic sight as one remembers that these heaps of ruins are the ruins of homes, and home in France to the French folk is at least as dear as home in England is to us.

81

I always try to visit the Church – that is, if it can be found. Sometimes I can't find it. The village Church is an outstanding feature of a French village just as it is in the village at home. For that reason it usually goes first. I have seen many village Churches in utter ruins. I visited one the other day. The roof and the walls were in one great heap in what was once the nave – that was all. In another I found midst the ruins of the fallen roof and shattered walls an altar still standing, with a statue of St. Peter. On the path outside were the broken pieces of stained glass from the windows. The churchyard Crucifix was broken, the tombstones smashed, and in many cases the graves had been blown open by shells. War does not respect holy places or holy things, nor do shells spare them. These Churches had been the spiritual homes of villagers for generations. Here they had been baptised and made their first Communion; here they went to Mass on Holy Days. The churchyards were the resting places of their dead. One cannot enter into the anguish of the villagers when one day they return again home.

I think two thoughts are in one's mind as one surveys the ruined homes and Churches of France. The first is a renewed determination to go on at whatever cost till the cruel invader of this country is beaten to his knees. The sufferings of France demand punishment and satisfaction. The people in England and elsewhere who talk about peace *now* forget that peace now means a peace of such a kind that the wrong will go unpunished, and the ruin unpaid for. We all want peace – no one more than the soldiers in the trenches, but the only peace worth having is a victorious peace – a peace resulting from the vindication of the right. For such a peace we urgently pray.

And then I think, too, that, as one sees the countryside ruined and desolate, one's thoughts turn to another countryside – the country towns and villages of England all peaceful and secure, and in that contrast there is much ground for gratitude to God, Who, far beyond our deserts, has spared us these horrors of war – the desolation of our homes and the ruin of our Churches. I wonder if people at home realise how much they have to be thankful for. England has her sufferings in this conflict, but this she has been spared.

I am,

Yours sincerely,

S. F. Leighton Green

Letter 20

[Probably written in the trenches near Lagnicourt, opposite the Hindenburg line, France] Oct. 5, 1917 [Friday 5 October 1917]

Dear People,

It seems a very long time since I was at St. Barnabas, and saw you all, but it is only just four weeks ago today that I left Norwich. It was a very great pleasure to be back again in the dear old Parish and to worship again with you in the dear old Church, and I wish to thank you for the kind welcome you gave me.

I am especially glad to know that the Mag-Fag Fund made a good push when I was with you. The concert I was able to attend was a great success, and although it was the second performance there was a full house. I am very much obliged to those who got the show up, and those who performed at it. I hear that there is to be another push later on. I hope you will support the second one as you did the first. The Mag-Fag Fund becomes more and more important as time goes on, and more and more useful, and I am very glad to have its help. I hope you will support Mr. Fraser, who so kindly manages the Fund, in every possible way.

Returning from leave is a very trying time. For the more you see of war the less you like it, and when you return from leave you return to trenches and shells, dirt, desolation and nasty smells. I was quite a long time finding my Battalion, as they had moved many miles during my leave in England. However, I was able to spend a Sunday in a vast base Camp, and see how things were worked there.[96] There are several Chaplains attached to the Camp permanently, and as they do not move about like the rest of us, they are able to put things on a more lasting basis. The Camp Church was a very beautiful one, quite new and recently consecrated by the Bishop of Khartoum.[97]

There were many Celebrations early on Sunday morning, and there seemed to be a fair number of Communicants. The Camp is a large city, with houses sufficient for the whole population of Norwich, so there were endless canteens, cinemas, recreation rooms and clubs. The Officers Club was a very fine one indeed, and is a Memorial to two brothers who have fallen in this war. For the first time I came across a large number of women and girls in the uniform of the Women's Army Auxiliary Corps. They were engaged chiefly as waitresses in the Club. They seemed happy in their work. I have no doubt they felt they were doing their bit, as indeed they were – feeding hungry officers.

83

After a day or two in the Camp I was ordered to entrain at 6.30 a.m. one morning to proceed to the rail-head of my Division. The train was a long one – there were horse boxes and luggage vans for the men, and broken down carriages, which had never been cleaned since the war began, for the officers. I am not sure which were more comfortably off. Ten hours in this train and a march of eight miles brought me to transport lines of my Battalion. I found it just on the move to the trenches, and there I joined them next day. Another leave over, but if, as the Americans say, the war is going on for another three years, I shall look forward to a few more. On the whole, in spite of their discomforts, and in spite of going back, they are worth while. My only wish is that the men in the ranks who do the fighting got more leave, for no one deserve it more than they do.

Recruiting poster for
Queen Mary's Army
Auxiliary Corps

With all good wishes.

I am,

Yours sincerely,

S. F. L. Green

Letter 21

[Probably written in rest billets at Frémicourt, Cambrai sector, France]
[Undated, probably written early November 1917]

Dear People,

Ever since I returned to France we have been living in that part of the country which, early this year, was evacuated by the Germans, as a result of the great battle of the "Somme." It is not a particularly comfortable part of France to live in, because before they retired, the Germans destroyed everything they possibly could. Every house and cottage was made uninhabitable by blowing down the sides and the roof. Every place which could afford any shelter, such as barns or outhouses, was treated in the same way. The roads were broken up, the bridges were broken down. The trees

84

were cut down across the roads, and the orchards were rendered fruitless for all time. The wells were poisoned, so that even now water has to be carried for many miles. In fact, everything was done to make life as dismal as possible for the British troops occupying this desolate area.

During the summer months the troops out of the line were able to live in tents, but now the winter is coming it has been necessary to build large camps of huts for their accommodation. The huts are made of wood and corrugated iron, and they shelter some thirty or forty men. They are very cold and comfortless at first sight, but the soldier, like all Englishmen, wherever he goes, makes his home, and so it is possible to see huts brightened up considerably after a few days. They have indeed to sleep on the floor, but that becomes an easy thing when you have to work hard as the British soldier does every day of his life. Anyhow life in the huts is luxury compared with life in the trenches, and very glad we are to get to them for six days after eighteen days spent in the line.

I have been reading just lately a book by a French soldier on his experience in the war.[98] He describes its various horrors, but in his opinion one of the worst is mud. I am not sure that every one would agree, but certainly one of the horrid things in war is mud. In this part of the country we have plenty of it. When it is fine, it is thick and slippery, and you flounder about in it, and are lucky if you do not fall. If it is wet, it becomes a dark slushy stream, and you wade through it; at times up to your knees. But wet or fine, there is mud everywhere. There are few more unpleasant experienced in life than floundering through mud and water in the dark. It is then you become what the soldiers call "fed up."

We have had rather wet weather out here of late, and wet weather first of all delays the progress of the war; and secondly it adds to its other discomforts. In the trenches the men build little shelters for themselves. They are roughly made with sandbags and bits of timber and iron. The wet and rain bring down the shelter, and the rest of the night has to be spent in the trench walking about in the rain. The trenches become little streams of liquid mud. The sides of the trenches begin to collapse. At night it begins to get cold and even frosty. The one great consolation is the nightly rum ration.[99]

There is one thing I want to say. Rightly or wrongly the men out here get the impression that people at home don't care a scrap what happens to men out here, so long as there are no air-raids, and everything goes on as usual there. Anyhow I wish people at home would do something to demonstrate the falsity of this impression. If when they go night by night to a comfortable bed they would remember the men in the trenches standing all night in the wet and cold, the slush and mud, I think that somehow they would not find

85

it impossible to get up early and go to Church to say a prayer at the altar for the soldiers. I wonder how many people go to the Friday Celebration with its special intention for those engaged in the war? And the weekly Intercession Service, what of that? And the people who cannot attend on week-days, are they more regular on Sundays?

A good Church lad of East London, who just returned from leave, said to me, "The people at home, why, they don't care a straw what happens out here. The halls (i.e., cinema and music halls) are fuller than ever, and the clergyman at Church says that only a very few turn up there. What do they care?"

Whether people at home realise it or not, the men in the trenches don't mind what they have to go through, if only the people at home care about them as they face the perils and hardships, discomforts and horrors of war. It is a thoroughly bad thing when they come to feel that people don't care. I hope you at St. Barnabas' will help all you can by your constant prayers. They need your help and deserve it too.

Yours sincerely,
S. F. L. Green

Letter 22

[Probably written in rest billets at Ecurie, Arras sector, France]
Advent III [Sunday 16 December 1917]

Dear People,

In the devastated parts of France, of which I told you in my last letter, it is not always easy for the Chaplains to carry on their work. The camps are usually very crowded, and it is practically impossible to get one of the huts I described for use as a Church.

Now that the winter has come Church Parade in the open-air is out of the question, and many of us are grateful to the Church Army and Y.M.C.A. for use of their huts for Church Parade and voluntary Services.

At the same time it often happens that there is no such hut, and in these places we have to do the best we can. Till quite recently we have been in the line for eighteen days, and then come out for six days' rest and training. The village to which we came was in ruins. The village Church apparently had been blown up by a mine. We lived in huts; there was no hut to spare for a Church. Consequently in this place we had to set to work to find a Church somehow. We discovered a ruined stable, and with the help of canvas, timber, and corrugated iron, we repaired it, and it became the Brigade

Church for several months. It gradually improved in appearance from week to week, as we were able to adorn and make it more worthy of its purpose. At the East end we had long curtains and an English Altar. The flower vases were just 18-pounder shell-cases polished. The candlesticks were also beaten out of old shell cases. The walls of the stable were covered with canvas and adorned with pictures. This stable, transformed into a Church, was our spiritual home for six days out of every twenty-four, and we were all sorry when we had to leave it. We hope that it is still used as a Church, but often these villages get overcrowded with troops, and then everything has to go to give them shelter, and the Church is lost. Only just recently I had an opportunity of visiting one of the Churches we built in a farm last summer in one of the villages. I hoped that it was a Church still, but I found that the barn was now in use for other purposes. The floor was covered with vegetables, and on the Altar I found a stock of cauliflowers!

I came across a disused trench just recently. It was falling into decay, as the line had been advanced for several hundred yards. The shelters and dugouts were falling in. Quite unexpectedly I came across a signboard with the words, "To St. Anselm's Church." I followed the direction, and at last came to St. Anselm's. A little white cross stood over a semi-circular, corrugated iron structure, built into the side of the trench, and covered with sandbags and earth. The entrance was very small, but I managed to get in somehow. St. Anselm's could hold twelve or fifteen men. The East end had an Altar cut out of the chalk. Round the walls were a few small picture-postcards – pictures of our Lord and His Mother and the Saints. There was also a notice-board which stated that St. Anselm's was erected by men of the Drake Battalion of the Royal Naval Division in memory of their fallen comrades, and that the first Service therein had been a Requiem on their behalf.[100] Trench Churches are not very common, but this was typical of those I have seen.

From all this you may gather that we sometimes long for the Churches at home. Maybe we only realise what a Church becomes to us when we no longer have the use of it, and have to make shift as best we can.

I am afraid this letter will arrive too late to wish you a Happy Christmas, but not too late to wish you all at St. Barnabas' a Happy New Year. I would beg of you to make a fresh start in doing all you can to help the men out here by your prayers at the Altar. There are serious days ahead of us. We shall be glad to feel that the praying line at home is supporting with all its strength the fighting line out here.

I am,
Yours sincerely,
S. F. Leighton Green

P.S. – I am grateful to you for cigarettes and Magazines duly received from Mr. Fraser. I hope the next push on behalf of the Mag. Fag Fund, which I hear comes off early in the New Year, will be strongly supported.

Letter 23

[Written in St Barnabas' Parish, Heigham, Norwich, England]
January, 1918 [written after Sunday 20 January 1918]

Dear People,

I am writing this letter in St. Barnabas' Parish. It is a very great joy to be back again, and to worship with you in our beautiful Church at the Festival of the Dedication. To one who has had to worship anywhere and under any conditions, it is a real happiness to come to St. Barnabas', and find the Church and services increasing in beauty, and the memory of this Festival will be a real help in the trying days to come.

I left my Battalion in rest billets – the first rest we have had for six months. We were marched to a village some twenty miles behind the line, and the sight of a village untouched by fire and other marks of war was a strange but pleasant one.[101] The billets of the men in barns and farmhouses are not exactly luxurious, but we look forward to unbroken nights and days of relaxation. The days when we are out at rest are the happiest we know in the time of war. A certain amount of training has to be gone through, but there are football matches and evening entertainments. There are warm estaminets where we can sit and smoke, and have coffee or "vin rouge" or a glass of French beer. The distant rumbling of the guns and the flashes in the sky at night remind us that there is still a war on, but for the most part men contrive to forget it during the period of rest. Doubtless we shall have a more active share in it again.

We spent our Christmas this year in the trenches, where there was anything but "peace on earth." I went out on Christmas Eve to provide service for troops behind the line and on Christmas morning I celebrated several times for little groups of men who came to make their Christmas Communion. Some of these services were held in strange places and under strange conditions, but in spite of all that, they were very real and helpful. Need I say how much the thoughts of the soldiers at Christmas time turn again home? Home means so much at Christmas, and Christmas can never be quite what it was until the guns are silent and the war is at an end.

On the Sunday after Christmas [30 December] we were out of the trenches, and had our Christmas Festival. Services in a Church Army Hut

88

with the Christmas hymns were, in the face of many difficulties, quite fairly well attended. On New Year's Day we had a Christmas Dinner, beef, vegetables, plum pudding, tinned fruit, cheese, apples, nuts and beer, all vanished with great rapidity and enthusiasm ran high. Everybody hoped that next year's Christmas dinner would be celebrated at home. Of course that is what every one has hoped for the last four years. However, we were all optimists, just at that moment. Only the pessimist murmured "What 'opes!"

Thank you for all the kindness of your welcome.

I am, Yours sincerely,

S. F. L. Green

Letter 24

[Probably written in the trenches near Oppy, Arras sector, France]
[Undated, but after 21 February 1918]

Dear People,

It seems a long time since I left St. Barnabas to return to the front. I have just realized that the usual, monthly effort is required for the Magazine. I have been writing these letters for over two years now, and I think it is time that some of our other soldiers from St. Barnabas' had a turn. I quite think that some of our boys in Palestine might record their experiences. I feel that you must all be getting tired of news from the western front. However, the Vicar has not given any orders to this effect, so here goes with my usual contribution.

I am back again with the Battalion once more. I found that my parish had grown in my absence. Many new officers and men had joined, and I was kept quite busy in trying to get to know them. A Battalion is always changing, unfortunately. Casualties, sick and wounded, make gaps which have to be filled. New drafts arrive, and the work of the Chaplain has to begin afresh.

On Ash Wednesday [13 February] we had a Confirmation. Some forty soldiers in the Division were confirmed by the Deputy Chaplain-General in a little wooden Church dedicated in honour of the Protomartyr St. Stephen. These Confirmations at the front are always very impressive. Life at the front with the very narrow margin between life and death makes for reality in religion. One has great hopes that the men confirmed out here, or rather such of them who are spared to return home, will bring into our Church life new vigour and strength when in God's good time Peace comes again.

Since I have been back I have often thought of St. Barnabas' as I saw it on the Festival of the Dedication. Since my return I have worshipped on Sunday in a Canteen, a Cinema and a barn, the two former very cold, and the latter very wet. In the barn, which was in a very out-of-the-way sort of place a long distance from the village Church, I celebrated the Holy Communion. A dear old peasant woman looked in and saw my rough Altar with its Crucifix and candles. A little later the soldiers came, and during the Celebration I saw the dear old thing kneeling at the back with her Prayer Book. She afterwards told me that she had not been able to get to the Church for months and months, so she thought she would come to the soldiers' Mass.

As I write this letter we are in the trenches once again.[102] At first they were very muddy, and in parts almost impassable, but now the severe frost has come again, so though it is very cold it is easier to get about. I think that most of us if we were asked to choose between being wet and being cold, would choose to be cold, so at the moment we are content. We are all waiting for we know not what. It can't be long before the peace time warfare of the trenches is over and the day of battle dawns.

Think of those waiting men in the trenches, keeping sleepless watch day and night, and I am sure your thoughts will pass into prayers on their behalf.

Yours sincerely,
S. F. L. Green

Letter 25

[Written in the trenches near Oppy, Arras sector, France]
Passion Week [between 24 and 28 March 1918]

Dear People,

The suggestion that some of the boys in Palestine or Mesopotamia should take a turn in writing the monthly war letter has not been approved, so as I have not been relieved yet, it is time I began to write another letter.

It is not easy at the Front to observe times and seasons, so I fear our Lenten observance is rather spasmodic. However, the Chaplains attempt to do what is possible in the way of special Services, and we try to exchange pulpits from time to time. Lent has been a season of great tension from a military point of view, and so many of our arrangements have fallen through at the eleventh hour. There has been strenuous work going on to strengthen the line and all our defences to be ready for all emergencies. As the result, Sunday has often been a strenuous working day, and so congregations were rather thin. The little Church of St. Stephen, I mentioned in one of my recent letters, has met with disaster. It was a wooden building set up for us by the Royal Engineers of our Division. A fortnight ago a shrapnel shell made seventy holes in the roof, several bullets lodged in the bellows of the harmonium, which was, temporarily at any rate, put out of action. The next day a shell landed just beside the Church, and blew in one of its sides. So you see that, like the Apostle, we are able to say "that a great door and effectual is opened unto us," but like him, we experience "many adversaries."[103] So much for the Ecclesiastical intelligence.

When you have nothing much to write about in letters there is always one subject on which to comment, viz., the weather. We have been having days of wonderful weather, considering that we are in the month of March. Early mornings have seemed like May, and afternoons have been as warm as summer. Weather matters a great deal to everybody. It is almost everything at times to soldiers. In odd corners we have come across daffodils, and the song of birds has alternated with the scream of shells. It is wonderful how birds carry on in the middle of a bombardment, unmoved by any fear or worry. They make their nests, rear their young, in the trench shelters occupied by the men, who take extraordinary care not to interfere with the happiness of these refugees of the trenches. I saw an interesting sight the other day. The trenches been rather heavily bombarded by the enemy, and the shells had evidently broke into the nest of a rat and her eight young. From the side of the trench I watched the mother rat carrying her young from shattered nest into a shell-hole just in No Man's Land. Eight journeys, and all the little rats were placed in safety. Further I could not see, but I imagine a nest was built in the shell-hole, and there they dwell in safety.

I need hardly say what anxious days and nights we have been passing through. Some day I hope to able to tell you more about them. They have been days of constant vigilance, with little sleep lest we should be off our guard when the day came. Well, as I write, it seems that the day of watching is giving place to the days of action. Things are just developing at this moment.[104] Once again I ask for your prayers for the men who hold the line.

With all good wishes for Easter and Eastertide.

I am,

Yours sincerely,

S. F. L. Green

Letter 26

Dear People,

When I wrote my last letter the great German offensive was just beginning, and from that day in Passion Week there has been continuous and severe fighting. During these weeks as you know our troops had to face the most overwhelming attacks of the enemy and for a time the position was extremely critical. The whole future of the Allied cause, and with it the future Liberties of mankind and all that we hold dear were trembling in the balance. There are severe ordeals, perhaps severer ordeals, yet to be faced. As the Commander-in-Chief in a special order of the day has told us we are fighting with our backs against the wall and we must fight it out now to the last man.[105] We are fighting for our homes, for liberty and righteousness in the world, for the safety and welfare of the generations yet unborn. In such a cause we should all be willing to fight and to suffer, and if need be to die. So much for the issues at stake in the great battle or series of battles, which are taking place in France today. I would to God that the men who are facing these powerful attacks upon our lines could feel that they were being upheld throughout these terrible days by the people at home – a nation on its knees. From all I learn, this is far from being the case. One would have thought that in the presence of such a conflict the world would have been awed, and that the people for whom such sacrifices were being made would be striving to be worthy of them. As I read the papers I see little signs that it is so. In Holy Week, I am told the music halls were crowded, the Churches were nearly empty. Truly a strange way of dealing with the present crisis.

In Passion Week and Holy Week we were engaged in continuous fighting of the severest kind, and in the section which we held the enemy attacks were substantially held, due under God to the gallant and determined spirit of the troops. I may not go into any details, but I don't think people at home can ever be thankful enough for the spirit of the British armies in the field. The overwhelming menace to the cause we champion has restored afresh the spirit and morale of the troops in a wonderful way. Whatever the issue may be no fault attaches to the fighting men. All that men could be they have been, all that we could do they have done. May God bless them for their efforts and give rest and peace to those who have fallen in the battle. The gallant deeds of these few weeks will be wonderful heartening records in the days to come. They are the real treasures of any people, and all our life is being enriched today by many deeds of self-sacrifice and devotion to duty.

On Easter Eve [30 March] we were taken out of the line, a weary and depleted crowd. We marched back to comparative safety, and it was possible to observe the Queen of Festivals. I had a Church Parade for my Battalion. We sang the Easter hymns, and at the conclusion the Brigadier-General Commanding addressed the troops, and thanked them for their good work in the previous week.[106] I celebrated several times for various units, and we had a fine number of communicants considering our depleted numbers. A voluntary Evensong was well attended and brought to a conclusion a very happy Easter Day.

Large reinforcements as you know have arrived in France, and in the next few days we were being re-formed with large new drafts of men. Most of them have served before and have wound stripes. Some were just lads of nineteen who have come out to do their duty at the earliest possible moment, and very keen boys they seem to be. In a few days we were on the move again and before Low Sunday [7 April] we were in the line.

Thank you very much for the kind resolution you passed at the Vestry. It was very kind of you to think of it. Send out parcel after parcel of cigarettes, they are always urgently needed.

Yours sincerely,

S. F. L. Green

Letter 27

[Probably written in rest billets at Dainville, Arras sector, France]
Whitsunday [Sunday 19 May 1918]

Dear People,

The troops I have the honour to serve have been constantly in the line since the time I wrote my last monthly letter. Consequently I have not very much to write about this month. It has been a very long spell of trench work, the artillery has been very active and there is continuous warfare going on in the air, but we have not seen anything of "Fritz," as the soldiers call him. However, in these days trench life is a very anxious matter. At no time did the men get very much rest in the trenches, but now they get less than ever, I think. The situation demands incessant watchfulness and a very sharp look-out over No Man's Land. Through the grey mist of the dawn the enemy might be launching another attack, and the line must be always ready. Constant watchfulness by day and night is the order of the day, and that means constant strain.

We have had some nasty nights of late. There are few nights more uncomfortable than those in which we move from one position to another. One night just recently we had to move. It was raining in torrents and there was a high wind. The country is broken up by shell fire and marked by huge shell holes. The tracks, little paths through the maze of wire entanglements and other impediments, become very slippery with wet and mud. Add to this that it was so dark that you could only be certain of the presence of the man in front of you by stretching out your hand to touch him. Then imagine lines of men in single file carrying packs, rifles, Lewis guns, rations, ammunition and goodness knows what else, starting off to a place they have never seen before, led by guides who because of the blackness of the night become doubtful of the way. Through the dark night over the wet and slippery paths, in among the shell holes now full of mud and water, we stagger on our way. There is much tumbling into holes, much tripping over wire, much slipping in the mud, much sweat and much more swearing (I fear) and after a few hours of this sort of thing we get there covered with mud and wet to the skin.

To-morrow night we shall be back again in the front line, and it will be many a long day before we get any more services. You will see in the paper that there is much tension and at any moment the second phase of the attack may begin. Life will be no picnic this year. Anyhow we know what we are up against. The strength of the enemy offensive and the humiliation of a German peace as revealed in the case of Russia and Roumania have combined to stiffen the morale of the troops. The issues at stake have become clear to the meanest intelligence. Defeat means ruin, sheer utter ruin, in every department of life. Compromise means this hell again one day. A victorious peace alone can save us from the former – a victorious peace alone can afford a prospect of averting the latter. Therefore when you say your prayers, pray for victory.

I have today received 6,000 cigarettes. They go with me to-morrow to the front line. I think with strict economy they may last three days! Keep Mr. Fraser in funds. We shall want an endless stream of parcels, a regular barrage of cigarettes to keep us going this summer.

Yours sincerely,
S. F. Leighton Green

Letter 28

[Probably written at rest billets in Dainville, Arras sector, France]
[Undated, probably written in July 1918]

Dear People,

It was a great pleasure to read the St. Barnabas' Magazine without being a contributor to its pages.[107] I found the news of the boys on the various battle fronts very interesting indeed, and I hoped that you would have said that you wanted such news continued. However, I fear you have let me down. I have received orders for a letter.

I am afraid there is very little to record, or rather very little that the Censor would allow to be recorded – quite a different matter, of course. Consequently I must fall back on topics of no military significance, and first of all, of course, the weather, though even that has military significance in many ways.

The early summer here has been very beautiful. Even in desolated areas like these battlefields in France summer makes a deal of difference. The wild flowers go on blooming in the coarse grass, and even old shell-holes become radiant with the scarlet of the poppy and the blue of the cornflower. In ruined villages the roses still bloom in the garden, and the blossoms on the chestnut along the roads have been quite wonderful to see. There has been very little rain for several weeks, and so trench life has been as little unpleasant as it is possible to be. We have had very long periods in the line this year, but the trenches have been dry and when you have to live and eat and sleep in them that is a matter of some consequence I can assure you. There are few things so damaging to morale as wet, water-logged trenches. Of course, life even so is not all honey. You read in the papers of much shelling activity. People at home probably think if no battle is raging that that does not mean very much, but it does when you live in the trenches which are being shelled. When the bays on either side of you have been blown in, and a dozen or so men killed or wounded, it is not quite easy for those who live in the middle bay to remain unmoved or preserve a complacent frame of mind. But such things happen every day and every night. I need hardly say, too, what an anxious thing it is in these days of sudden great attacks to hold the line at all. The constant vigilance and preparedness required is in itself the greatest possible strain.[108]

However, if we hold the line for longer periods than ever, at last we get relief for a few days, and we make the most of them. It is something to get an unbroken night's rest, and it is something to get a real hot bath. In these short periods, of course, everything is done to "buck things up," as the saying is. The Divisional Concert Party, the Divisional Band all get a move on to amuse the troops, and very excellent institutions they both are. Quite recently we had an afternoon sports in the Brigade, where every one for the time being forgot all about the War. These days go all too quickly, and then it is time to go up the line again.

I have received some good parcels of cigarettes. They are particularly useful in such days as theses. Please keep the fund going.

Yours sincerely,

S. F. L. Green.

Letter 29

[Probably written in billets at Grand Rullecourt, France]
[Undated, but written after Tuesday 20 August 1918]

Dear People,

Since I last wrote to you we have been keeping a great anniversary – the fourth Anniversary of our entry into the war. At home, I see, the day, which fortunately came on a Sunday, was marked by many remarkable public acts of devotion. Out here, under the conditions imposed by war, everything possible was done to observe the Day of Remembrance. The Army Headquarters arranged a service at which every unit in this particular Army was represented, French, American and Portuguese. The Deputy Chaplain-General, Dr. Gwynne, Bishop of Khartoum, preached the sermon, an address was also given by the Army Commander.[109] The troops I serve with were, unfortunately, in the front line, so we had no opportunity for service on that day, but I hear most battalions wherever they were kept August 4 as a special time of thanksgiving and resolve.

Since I last wrote a great change has been effected in the military situation out here. The great victory on the Marne secured the safety of Paris and the push made by the British troops is regarded as a definite guarantee of the safety of the important city of Amiens.[110] In other words the extreme tension of the last five or six months is considerably relaxed. There may be much hard fighting ahead of us, but Germany has done her worst and, as the Commander-in-Chief has said, her effort has failed. We feel that a great crisis in the affairs of the Allies is over and that we can look forward to ultimate victory in God's good time. There have been and still are I believe, people who affirm that no military decision is possible in this war. A military decision is the only possible ending if the aims and objects of the Allies are to

96

be realised. So we must "hold fast." We must go on praying that the right may triumph, that God may give us the victory in the end.

Since I last wrote we have been a fortnight out of the line – the first time we have been out since the New Year. We had to march for three days in very hot and close weather – a very great ordeal for troops who have been in trenches for eight months. However, we got settled at last in a camp in a very pleasant village near some woods.[111] Although much training had to be done it seemed like a holiday after all those long months. There were no shells, and only the distant roar of the guns by day and sometimes the droning of a German raiding squadron overheard to show that there was still a war.

I am much obliged to you for the parcel of cigarettes and magazines. We can't have too many of them. In these days the canteens have not been very well supplied and your parcels have often saved the situation. Please keep Mr. Fraser well in funds. I keep on worrying him for parcels. I hope you will support him under the heavy burden I throw upon him and his fund.

Yours sincerely,
S. F. L. Green

Letter 30

[Probably written near Rumaucourt, Canal du Nord sector, France]
17th Sunday after Trinity [Sunday 22 September 1918]

Dear People,

First I want to say what a pleasure it was to be back again at S. Barnabas' and see you all. It is a real joy to be in a Church on a Sunday, and especially a beautiful Church like S. Barnabas'.[112] I was delighted to see the War Shrine in the North Aisle, and I hope that many of the faithful will go there to say their prayers for us out here, as well as to remember the gallant men and boys who have fallen in the Field of Honour.

Last Sunday I worshipped with you in Church – today I have been worshipping under different conditions. I found my battalion living in shell holes with such covering as they secure from waterproof sheets, scraps of iron, and bits of timber. The Holy Communion was celebrated in a trench with an improvised roof. It was very wet and very windy, and the lights on the Altar could not be kept burning. However, it was the best we could do, and I thought of you all at S. Barnabas'.[113]

I must thank you once again on behalf of my men for the push on behalf

97

of the Mag.-Fag Fund. I found that cigarettes were none too plentiful on my return, and I have already written to Mr. Fraser for a parcel.

Thank you for all the kindness of your welcome.

Yours sincerely,

S. F. L. Green

Letter 31

[Probably written in rest billets in Arras, Pas de Calais, France]
[Undated, probably written mid-October 1918]

Dear People,

We have been living lately in villages which have been occupied by the enemy for quite four years. They were situated miles behind his famous line of defences. Here his divisions came out to rest, and here he had his hospitals and convalescent depôts. The villages are badly damaged as the result of the fighting which took place before the Germans went, but they are not totally destroyed. In fact, we have better billets than we have had for many a long day. The village Churches have for the most part suffered considerable damage, and have been stripped of all their ornaments. I went the other day into a house quite close to a village church. It was the house the Curé. I found his library. His books had been thrown all over the floor; the cupboards and desks had all been smashed, and everything was in indescribable disorder. The vestments and decorations of the Church had all been thrown about the place, trampled under foot, and hopelessly ruined. It is not pleasant to have enemy forces resident in your village.[114]

There is every evidence to show that the Germans had no intention of leaving these pleasant villages so quickly. He had been preparing to make himself comfortable for the winter. There were great dumps of coal and felled trees near most of them, and it was clear that, whoever else was going to be cold he certainly was not. The hospitals he had were very comfortable places, and seemed to be well stocked with all the necessaries for hospital life.[115] The billets of the German soldiers were well furnished with beds, tables, and chairs, the property of poor French civilians, who must have had very little left for their own use. They probably had to sleep in the attics and the cellars. In almost every village we found a German cemetery, where the German soldiers who died in hospital had been buried. We found also the graves of many British soldiers who had died of wounds in German hands. These graves are all being registered by our Graves Commission, and every effort will be made to preserve them.[116]

98

The advances made in recent weeks have often been very rapid, and we are often short of that essential commodity – Cigarettes. Your parcels of fags will be doubly welcome in these hard times.

> With best wishes,
>> Yours sincerely,
>>> S. F. L. Green

An army chaplain tending British graves

Letter 32

> [Written in Douchy, Nord, France]
> [Undated, probably written on Saturday 2 November 1918]

Dear People,

At the present moment we are in a French village which eight days ago was occupied by German troops.[117] The French people were left behind, as the Germans had to go in the night in a very great hurry. The joy of the people is unbounded as they realise that their harsh captivity is over, and that they are now surrounded by friends. Our people have many stories to tell of their treatment by the Germans. It appears that in this particular village, a long way behind the German lines, the people were not badly treated by the ordinary German soldiers, but they speak with intense hatred of the German officers and especially the local town commandant. They seem to have been treated with great severity, and for every little breach of the law they were heavily fined. At times they have been kept very short of food, and there is no doubt that they have suffered very severely in health as the result. Today I witnessed a very pathetic scene: the return of a French soldier to his home after four years' absence. He was called up to the Colours in August, 1914. He had to leave wife and children behind in the village; and very shortly after he left the Germans came, and have been here till October, 1918. He had not heard anything of them all that time, but as soon as he knew the British troops had recovered the place he applied for leave, and it was granted. It was a very tearful but joyful scene, from which we hurried away with the feeling that the struggle of the British Army had not been fruitless.

On All Saints' Day [Friday, 1 November], as there was no opportunity to hold any service ourselves, I went to the village church, where the dear old Curé, who had stayed here with his flock all through the years of the German occupation, sang the Mass. About 150 people, including the soldiers and the family I have told you of, attended. Two thin and pale little boys served at the Altar, and an old man played the rather broken-down organ. However, it was a very joyful service, and a very happy congregation. The old Curé preached a short sermon from the Altar steps, in which he spoke of the arrival of the British Army which had secured their freedom. Truly All Saints' Day, 1918, must have been to these village folk a day of peace on earth. Do keep up the Mag-Fag Fund. Yours is the sole supply to the Battalion. Push out parcel after parcel, if you please.

Yours sincerely,
S. F. L. Green

Letter 33

Near Maubeuge
[written in billets at Villers-sire-Nicole, nr Maubeuge, Nord, France]
4/12/18 [Wednesday 4 December 1918]

Dear People,
Since I last wrote to you many great and wonderful things have happened. From All Souls' Day [1 November] onward we were engaged in fighting the rear guards of the German Army, and so rapid was our advance that it was becoming almost impossible for us to keep contact with our rations. The railroads behind us were destroyed, and the roads had been blown up, and for one or two days the only possible way of getting our rations was for aeroplanes to drop sacks of food for the men, who were still

100

pursuing the retreating enemy. We received a tremendous welcome from the Belgian people.[118] For over four years they had been in the hands of their conquerors, and now they had seen them running away and they welcomed their deliverers with extra-ordinary signs of joy. The women rushed out and embraced the troops, filling their hands with souvenirs, and offering them coffee. The old men took off their hats, and bowed to us, shouting, "Vive l'Angleterre."

Then a few days later, when we were fairly exhausted after advancing and fighting daily for eight or nine days, news came of the impending armistice, and early on November 11 we had a telegram to say that hostilities would cease at 11 a.m. We were all dead tired and worn out, but it was with a great sigh of relief that we heard that the enemy had accepted the terms, and that the fighting was over. We ended the war in sight of the place when the British troops first went into action in August 1914, and there were some men in the Division who remembered the first German shell coming over.

On Sunday we had our Thanksgiving Services. True we had to have them out in the cold, but you can imagine what those Services meant to men who had seen it through. The Brigadier-General made a splendid speech to the men, laying emphasis on the fact that our gratitude was due to the God of our fathers, Who alone was the Giver of all Victory.

We had hoped that we should go to Germany as part of the Army of Occupation, but, for the present, we are doing garrison duty on the frontiers of France. Cigarettes are still very short, and books and papers more valuable than ever, so I hope you will keep Mr. Fraser in funds.

Before you receive this you will have kept Christmas, and hailed the Prince of Peace, but I shall be in time to wish you – and it seems more real since the victory is won, doesn't it – a very Happy New Year.

Yours sincerely,

S. F. L. Green

Letter 34

[Written in billets at Villers-sire-Nicole, nr Maubeuge, Nord, France]

[Undated, probably written mid-January 1919]

Dear People,

Since I last wrote another Christmas has come and gone, and I think that all our men would tell you it was the best Christmas they have spent in France. We did not sing our hymns to the harsh music of the guns, nor did we live in cold and desolate trenches, and much of the happiness here was

101

due to this, that this Christmas without war was the pledge of a better Christmas next year at home, with peace restored to a weary world. The cessation of hostilities gave us a better chance to make ready for the Festival. The woods around the village provided evergreens and holly in abundance, and mistletoe found its way into every billet. Whether the mistletoe witnessed the traditional rite I know not. May be the French girls here could tell you. Anyway the billets were bright with Christmas decorations, and the tables well supplied with Christmas fare. We waited many days in trepidation lest our order of turkey, pork, puddings, fruit, and all the other good things should not arrive in time. Alarming stories of a breakdown on the railways, and of lorries firmly fixed in mud, were in circulation; but on Christmas Eve they all rolled up, and the success of Christmas was assured. The men had their dinner at midday – a room for each company – and officers and sergeants waited upon them. There was much enthusiasm and afterwards much content with life in general and peace with all the world.

I had a very busy Christmas morning from 6 a.m. till noon. The Church parades were very hearty, with the old-time spirit, and the Christmas hymns; and the Celebrations of the Holy Communion were better attended than ever before.

Some one quite lately wrote and suggested that there could not be much to do now, so I might as well come home. Well, this is what I do just now. I am Chaplain to nearly 4,000 men scattered over many square miles, and on Sundays I have seven or eight Services to conduct. I have a weekly Bible Class, and a Guild of Communicants; I manage a Library; I run a Canteen; I sub-edit a Magazine; I conduct a Debating Society; I teach Latin for three hours a week; and now I have a Confirmation Class. No, there is nothing much to do!

I need hardly say how anxious every one is to get home, but it is no good getting impatient. We have won the War, but we have not yet won the Peace. People at home and men out here must see the thing through, and after all we have gone through, and all it has cost, we must not risk the great fruits of our labour – the settlement of a just and lasting Peace. I am much obliged for the cigarettes Mr. Fraser has sent. I hope you will keep the fund going for a few weeks, as you know an abundance of cigarettes produces content of mind.

With all good wishes for the New Year.

Yours sincerely,

S. F. L. Green

Letter 35

Dear People,

When I last wrote I had little expectation that I should be writing the next letter for the Magazine in England. However, it is often the unexpected that happens, and I am glad to be again at St. Barnabas', and I hope it will not be long before I am able to begin work again in real earnest.

I am myself very thankful that the Battalion to which I was attached is now no longer in existence. The process of demobilisation went on very rapidly in January, and nearly every day we had to say good-bye to the men who were proceeding to England. Church parades and other meetings became rapidly thinner every week. When I left there were about 100 men, who were going to the Rhine, and the rest would be gradually sent to England.

The gradual disappearance of the Battalion was rather a sad business in some ways. Those of us who had belonged to it for a long time could not help some feelings of regret as it gradually ceased to be. However, we have to accept the inevitable, and I hear, as I am writing, that the 1/4th London Regiment is no more.[119] I must confess that it was a trying time when I had to go round the billets to say good-bye to the remnants of the Battalion before I left. One had shared so many experiences of various kinds with these men, and the kind of experience for the most part which tends to bind men together. We are all hoping that we shall have opportunities for reunion in the days to come and we are all looking forward to annual meetings in London in the piping days of peace. Anyhow, looking back on it all, I shall always be proud to have been attached to so splendid a fighting unit as the London Fusiliers.

The journey back to England was a long one.[120] I had to come from the famous town of Mons to Calais. The journey, however, was very interesting, as we passed over the old familiar battlefields of Vimy and Arras. Very desolate they looked – these wrecked areas of France. One could not help wondering how all these devastated areas could hope to be redeemed, but the French are wonderful people, who get on with the job with tremendous enthusiasm. They are people who love the soil, and it will be very interesting to see what they accomplish in the way of rebuilding their towns and villages, and reclaiming the land. However, the journey came to an end at last, and we arrived at the base. There were crowds of cheering men waiting for the boats to sail, to bring them back to civil life and home. A novel feature of the journey across the Channel was the fact that our ship had no destroyers as an escort. The German Fleet is safely guarded at Scapa Flow.[121] So we got to England – safely home at last.

I should like to thank you for two things: –

(1) I know that in your prayers in Church, and I am sure in the case of many of you, in your prayers at home, you have remembered me and my work. All I can say now is, "Thank you." Your prayers have not been in vain; the thought of them has often been a help to me.

(2) In the practical sympathy you have always given to my work in the Mag-Fag Fund. To all who have kept it going by their subscriptions, and to Mr. Fraser who so kindly managed the Fund, I am very grateful and so is many a soldier whom you will never know.

I am,

Yours sincerely,

S. F. L. Green

The 4th Battalion, London Regiment, marching past the Mansion House, London, during the Victory Parade of 5 July 1919. Is Green in there somewhere?

Bibliography

Bickersteth, John (ed.), *The Bickersteth Diaries, 1914–1918* (London, 1995)

Burkill, Terry, *St Barnabas Church Heigham, Norwich. A Brief History and Guide* (Norwich, 2001)

Green, S. F. L., *The Happy Padre. Letters of the Rev. S. F. Leighton Green, M.C., C.F., 1916–1919* (Norwich, 1929)

Grimwade, F. Clive, *The War History of the 4th Battalion, The London Regiment (Royal Fusiliers), 1914–1919* (London, 1922; reprinted 2002)

Hankey, Donald, *A Student in Arms*, 17th edn (London, 1918)

London Evening News (ed.) *The Best 500 Cockney War Stories* (London, 1921)

Louden, Stephen H., *Chaplains in Conflict. The Role of Army Chaplains since 1914* (London, 1996)

Reading, Eric, *All Saints Parish Church, Mundesley. A History and Guide* (Mundesley, 1999)

Tiplady, Thomas, *The Kitten in the Crater* (London, 1917)

Wheeler-Holohan, A. V. and Wyatt, G. M. G., *The Rangers' Historical Records: From 1859 to the Conclusion of the Great War* (London, 1921)

Whitehead, Ian R., *Doctors in the Great War* (Barnsley, 1999)

Wilkinson, Alan, *The Church of England and the First World War* (London, 1978; reprinted 1996)

Other printed sources

Church Times; Crockford's Clerical Directory; Eastern Daily Press; Eastern Evening News; London Gazette; Norfolk Chronicle; Norwich Mercury; St. Barnabas', Heigham, Parish Magazine; The Times; The War Illustrated.

Notes

1 *Eastern Daily Press*, 6 June 1929. The author of this letter, 'E. P. M. M.', was Capt E. P. M. Mosely, who served with Green during the war.

2 Quoted in T. Burkill, *St Barnabas Church, Heigham, Norwich: A Brief History and Guide*, p. 6.

3 Lanchester family papers (Norfolk Record Office, ref. MC 634).

4 *St Barnabas' Parish Magazine*, September 1914.

5 The 1st Norwich Battalion was officially recognised as a cadet force of the King's Royal Rifle Corps on 11th July 1914; Green and Lanchester were both Assistant Chaplains of the Battalion (Norfolk Record Office, ref. SO 206).

6 Quoted in A. Wilkinson, *The Church of England and the First World War*, p. 254.

7 *Our Glorious Heritage. A Book of Patriotic Verse for Boys and Girls*, compiled by Charles Seddon Evans (London, 1914), pp. ix–x.

8 *St Barnabas' Parish Magazine*, September 1914.

9 John Taylor Smith (1860–1938), former bishop of Sierra Leone, appointed Chaplain-General in 1901.

[10] Information from Green's interview card quoted courtesy of the Trustees of the Museum of Army Chaplaincy, Amport, Hampshire.

[11] 'Bristow' was probably the Revd Walter Ewart Bristow, vicar of St Paul's, Northampton, who had been an army chaplain at Aldershot and Malta before the war (information from Crockford's). the association of 'mincing' with effeminacy would not have been as explicit in 1916 as it later became.

[12] St Barnabas' register of services, 1914–18 (Norfolk Record Office, ref. PD 470/21).

[13] Information from I. R. Whitehead, *Doctors in the Great War*.

[14] 'The Padre's Work', *The Times*, 25 March 1918.

[15] Quoted from his diaries published in *Rupert Edward Inglis, Chaplain to the Forces, Rector of Frittenden*, privately printed *c.* 1920.

[16] Harry William Blackburne (1878–1963) became an army chaplain in 1903.

[17] The Revd Blackburne's comments are from his notebooks, used courtesy of the Trustees of the Museum of Army Chaplaincy.

[18] The citation, dated 13 November and signed by the Commander in Chief, Field Marshal Sir Douglas Haig, was published in the *London Gazette* on 2 January 1917.

[19] *The War Illustrated*, 3 February 1917, p. 600.

[20] No.18 Squadron's FE2b biplanes, built by Boulton & Paul of Norwich, were tested on Mousehold Heath in 1915.

[21] The 4th Battalion, London Regiment, was gradually expanded into four battalions, the 1/4th (first fourth), 2/4th, 3/4th and 4/4th, the last two being reserve cadres that did not serve overseas.

[22] Review of *The War History of the 4th Battalion, The London Regiment* in *The Times*, 12 September 1922.

[23] D. Hankey, *A Student in Arms*, pp. 240–1.

[24] Green preached at St Barnabas' on 4 March 1917 (Norfolk Record Office, ref. PD 470/21).

[25] F. C. Grimwade, *The War History of the 4th Battalion, The London Regiment*, p. 263.

[26] J. Bickersteth (ed.), *The Bickersteth Diaries*, p. 170.

[27] On the first Sunday, 28 August 1917, Green gave a sermon on the war at a memorial service at St Barnabas' for local soldiers Sapper Percy Mower, Sgt Thomas Tubbs and Pte Walter Pitcher.

[28] *St Barnabas' Parish Magazine*, October 1917.

[29] Wilkinson, ibid., pp. 100–1.

[30] Grimwade, ibid., p. 341.

[31] *St Barnabas' Parish Magazine*, July 1919.

[32] *St Barnabas' Parish Magazine*, February 1918 and Norfolk Record Office, ref. PD 470/21.

[33] *London Evening News* (ed.), *The Best 500 Cockney War Stories*.

[34] Grimwade, ibid., p. 403.

[35] *St Barnabas' Parish Magazine*, May 1918.

[36] Norfolk Record Office, ref. PD 470/21.

[37] *London Gazette*, 9 December 1919, p. 22.

[38] Grimwade, ibid., p. 503.

[39] *St Barnabas' Parish Magazine*, December 1918.

[40] *St Barnabas' Parish Magazine*, March 1919.

[41] Grimwade, ibid., p. 506.

[42] National Archives, Kew, ref. WO 374/28994.

[43] Philip 'Tubby' Clayton (1885–1972) and Neville Talbot (1879–1943).

[44] *St Barnabas' Parish Magazine*, June 1920.

[45] Mundesley had in fact a recent evangelical history. Before the war it had hosted annual Bible Conferences, organised by Nonconformist preacher, the Revd Dr George Campbell Morgan of Westminster Chapel. The rector at this period, Revd Tegg Harvey, was Low Church. The appointment of an Anglo-Catholic as his successor must have been controversial.

[46] *Eastern Evening News*, 31 May 1929.

[47] His grave originally had a simple oak kerb, which decayed over time and was not renewed. A chancel screen, with a crucifix and figures of the Virgin Mary and the Apostle John, was erected in the church in December 1929 to the memory of Green and Tegg Harvey. In 1931, Green's successor. The Revd Dr T. J. Williams-Fisher, a strict evangelical, went with workmen into the church and had the figures, which he regarded as idolatrous, sawn off. The Consistory Court later condemned his act as illegal and ordered that the figures be reinstated.

[48] Green's first letter from Flanders has not been found.

[49] Green's misspelling of trestles as 'tressels' has been retained.

[50] No doubt from the vicar, the Revd Lanchester, who served with a Red Cross ambulance brigade in France in 1915.

[51] Mr Fraser seems to have been a member of St Barnabas' congregation, though not a warden or sidesman.

[52] CCS 22 moved from Aire to Bruay early in April 1916. Green describes the move in Letter 4.

[53] Lena Ashwell, English actress and impresario who organised hundreds of concert parties for troops on the Western Front and further afield, often performed in primitive conditions within sight and sound of battle.

[54] J.T.Varden, churchwarden at St Barnabas' for twenty years.

[55] The Merry Knuts were a St Barnabas' church amateur dramatic group.

[56] The coal-mining town that CCS 22 moved to at the beginning of April 1916 was Bruay. The French had handed over this part of the front line to the BEF in March.

[57] The Feast Day of St Barnabas is celebrated on 11 June, the day on which this letter was written.

[58] It has not been possible to identify this man. No Royal Engineer sapper is known to have died at Bruay at this period.

[59] The Distinguished Conduct Medal was issued to other ranks for gallantry in the field. The Artois Offensive was launched by the British First Army near Neuve Chapelle on 9 May 1915.

[60] Possibly Pte William Henry Fisher, Liverpool Regiment, who died of wounds at Bruay on 24 April 1916, aged 20.

[61] Officially, soldiers had to be at least 19 to serve overseas, but there were in fact thousands as young as 17 and even younger at the front, a fact that many in the Army and society generally turned a blind eye to.

[62] This was the 17th Battalion, Middlesex Regiment, known as the 1st Footballers' Battalion because of the large number of professional footballers in its ranks. The only corporal of the 17th Middlesex to have been buried at Bruay military cemetery at this period was Albert Victor Butler from West Hampstead, Middlesex, who died of wounds on 13 May 1916. It isn't known what football club he played for, though it was presumably a London one.

[63] The Derby Scheme was a voluntary recruitment scheme introduced in 1915 prior to compulsory conscription. This casualty may have been Harry Wardman or John Owen

Wright, both Yorkshire Regiment privates who died of wounds, both aged 20, at Bruay on 12 and 13 May 1916 respectively.

[64] The Ward of St George was St Barnabas' boys' confirmation class. These men, all from the parish of Heigham, Norwich, were Cpl George Hardingham, 8th Battalion, Norfolk Regiment, died 1 July 1916; Pte Percy George Syder, 1st Canadian Battalion (Western Ontario Regiment), died 13 June 1916; Rifleman Cecil Pepper, 16th Battalion, King's Royal Rifle Corps, died 15 July 1916; and Pte Herbert Harvey, 8th Battalion, Norfolk Regiment, died 20 July 1916.

[65] This was RFC Squadron No. 18, stationed at Bruay 1 April to 22 July 1916 and again in August. Their two-seater FE2b 'pusher' biplanes were mainly used for photographic reconnaissance work.

[66] Possibly at the Battle of Neuve Chapelle, 10–13 March 1915, or later during the Artois Offensive in May.

[67] This RFC observer was almost certainly 2nd Lt James Mitchell, an Irish-Canadian officer serving with No. 18 Squadron, who died on 26 April 1916 aged 34. Mitchell was killed on a photographic reconnaissance patrol by a burst of machine-gun fire from a Fokker. The pilot, 2nd Lt J. C. Callaghan, was forced to land and survived.

[68] This incident occurred on the night of 15/16 July 1917. In fact, while 2nd Lt H. W. Butterworth was killed, the other pilot, Capt J. H. F. McEwan, although badly injured, survived, was taken prisoner and eventually handed over to neutral Holland.

[69] Green was on leave in Norwich on Sunday 1 October 1916 and preached at St Barnabas' (Norfolk Record Office, ref. PD 470/21).

[70] The National Mission of Repentance and Hope was launched by the Church of England in the autumn of 1916.

[71] Llewellyn Henry Gwynne (1863–1957), former bishop of Khartoum, was appointed Deputy Chaplain-General in July 1915.

[72] 'Soldiers of Christ Arise' is a hymn by Charles Wesley.

[73] Green transferred to the 168th Brigade, 56th (London) Division, then in the Neuve Chapelle sector, on 3 December 1916.

[74] This was probably the village of Laventie, where the 168th Brigade had their rest billets during the winter of 1916/17.

[75] One of Green's battalions was presumably the 1/4th London Regiment. The other was possibly the 1/12th London Regiment (Rangers), which was later chaplained by the Revd Julian Bickersteth. The history of the Rangers mentions Bow Bells' concerts in Laventie at this period: 'and ever and anon the Padre got up a regimental concert in that little hall by the shell-torn church' (A. V. Wheeler-Holohan and G. M. G. Wyatt, *The Rangers' Historical Records*, p. 84).

[76] The 1/4th Londons were in rest billets at Bout Deville at Christmas 1916.

[77] Christmas Eve, 1916, was on a Sunday, the day when compulsory Church Parades were held.

[78] John Merbecke, 16th-century English liturgist.

[79] This was a cartoon by Capt Bruce Bairnsfather. It was actually captioned 'Dear – At present we are staying at a farm …'.

[80] This was 'The Dug-out; A Memory of Gallipoli' a satirical poem by Lt A. P. Herbert (1890–1971), who went on to write 'Misleading Cases', a famous series of comic stories about the law.

[81] This was the village of Achicourt.

[82] Green omits to mention that he was wounded by shrapnel during this bombardment.

[83] The 56th Division were engaged in the opening action of the Arras Offensive, the First Battle of the Scarpe, and its aftermath at this period (9–21 April 1917).

[84] The Battle of the Somme, which began 1 July 1916.

[85] The German line occupied Neuville Vitasse in this sector.

[86] The words, slightly misquoted, are from Rupert Brooke's famous war poem 'The Soldier'.

[87] Pte John Moore, 2nd Battalion, Norfolk Regiment, died in Mesopotamia (Iraq), 24 February 1917.

[88] The 1/4th Battalion withdrew to rest billets in the village of Bayencourt on 21 April 1917. It had been billeted here in May 1916 before the Battle of the Somme.

[89] The Battalion moved to new billets in Gouy-en-Artois on 24 April 1917, then to Arras and into the assembly trenches on 2 May.

[90] The Revd Edward St. George Schomberg, a former curate at St Barnabas'. He was now vicar of Norton St Philip, Somerset. The Battalion was in billets in Arras at this date.

[91] This was almost certainly the 7th Battalion, Norfolk Regiment, which suffered heavily during the Battle of Arras.

[92] The Battalion marched to new billets in Berneville on 19 May 1917.

[93] The other of these notes and the end of this letter has not survived.

[94] Lt-Col. H. Campbell was the 1/4th Battalion's CO, 20 April to 14 August 1917. He was badly wounded in the 3rd Ypres Offensive and replaced by Lt-Col. A. F. Marchment, who remained its CO to the end of the war.

[95] Sapper Percy William Elves Mower, Royal Engineers, died 18 July 1917.

[96] This 'vast base Camp' was almost certainly at Etaples.

[97] The Deputy Chaplain-General, Bishop Gwynne.

[98] The book was *Le Feu: Journal d'une escouade* by Henri Barbusse, published 1916. An English translation, *Under Fire: the story of a squad*, was published in 1917. However, as Green knew French he may have been reading the original.

[99] The official history of the 4th London Regiment notes how the men were depressed one night when their rum jars were found to contain lime juice.

[100] The 1st (Drake) Battalion were part of the 189th Brigade, 63rd (Royal Naval) Division at this time. They fought at Ypres in October and November 1917.

[101] This was the village of Monchy Breton.

[102] The 1/4th Battalion went into the trenches near Oppy on 22 February 1917, after nine days in rest billets at the divisional reserve camp in Roclincourt.

[103] The text is from I Corinthians 16:9.

[104] The German spring offensive fell on the Oppy sector in the early hours of 28 March 1918. Green was with HQ Company in a position known as 'Ouse Alley' at this critical moment.

[105] Field Marshall Haig issued his famous 'to the last man' order on 11 April 1918. Green's next sentence is a paraphrase of that order.

[106] Brig.-Gen. Loch at Monchy Breton.

[107] There was no letter from Green in the June issue of *St Barnabas' Parish Magazine*.

[108] During May, June and July, while in the Tilloy-area trenches, the 1/4th Londons lost fourteen killed and forty-one wounded, which were officially considered 'light' casualties.

[109] This was possibly General Sir Julian Byng, commander of the Third Army.

[110] The 2nd Battle of the Marne, an Allied victory, ended around 3 August 1918. The Allied Amiens Offensive was launched on the 8th.

[111] The 1/4th Battalion left its billets in Berneville on 17 August 1918 and marched in stages over three days to billets in Grand Rullecourt.

[112] Green preached in St Barnabas' on Sunday 15 September 1918 (Norfolk Record Office, ref. PD 470/21).

[113] This camp was in the railway sidings at Feuchy.

[114] The liberated village Green describes was probably Ecourt-St Quentin in the Canal du Nord sector.

[115] The official regimental history notes that the German's hospitals were 'hard up for bandages' and had been tearing up curtains and paper as substitutes (Grimwade, ibid., p. 491).

[116] The Graves Registration Commission was established in March 1915 to record the place of burial of all British and Commonwealth service personnel. It was later known as the Imperial (now Commonwealth) War Graves Commission.

[117] This was the village of Douchy near Valenciennes in Nord. The 1/4th Battalion left here on 2 November 1918.

[118] The 1/4th Battalion marched through the liberated Belgian villages of Autreppe, Blaugies and La Dessoue near Mons on 8–10 November 1918, and was in billets in Sars-la-Bruyère on Armistice Day.

[119] A cadre of about fifty men of the 1/4th Battalion returned to London on 21 May 1919, where the unit was finally dispersed. It was revived as a London Territorial battalion in 1920. There was also an Old Comrades Association, of which Green was made president in 1929, shortly before his death. Members of this association officiated at his funeral.

[120] Green left for England on 13 February 1919, exactly three years after leaving for Flanders for the first time.

[121] Ships of the German High Seas fleet were scuttled by their own crews in Scapa Flow on 21 June 1919.

Index